PRAISE FOR *BLOSSOM*

"Carolin's book accompanies you like a close friend on the most important journey of all—coming home to yourself. How breath-giving to know that you can recover your wholeness after trauma, and even more, blossom into the life you deeply desire. Carolin's beautifully written and intimate chapters welcome all aspects of you into a new world of fulfillment and connection."

—Kathlyn Hendricks, Ph.D., BC-DMT
Co-author of *Conscious Loving*
and *The Conscious Heart*

"This is not a theoretical book on how to reclaim your power and heal your traumatic past. The 7 Step Journey is a call to action for anyone who wants to live an emotionally, spiritually and physically whole and fulfilling life."

—Janet Bray Attwood
New York Times Bestselling
Author, *The Passion Test*

"Carolin Hauser bravely approaches a sensitive subject with the tenderness and wisdom that can only come from personal experience. A book that comes from the heart for the heart."

—Michael Brown
author of *The Presence Process*
and *Alchemy of the Heart*

Blossom

Your 7-Step Journey to
Healing Childhood Sexual Abuse
and Creating Your Dream Life!

Carolin Hauser

This book is dedicated to my living children; my daughter Maja Rumi and my son Nouri Zen, and to all the children of this world. May you live safely as children, able to preserve your goodness and open heartedness so that you can grow up into the next generation of strong and loving adults that will bring forth a more peaceful world.

Table of Contents

Preface

Thank you for trusting in your gut and picking up this book. I am so glad *Blossom* made it into your hands.

If you have experienced childhood sexual abuse or any other trauma that has kept you from having lasting love and intimacy, and the life you want, *Blossom* is for you.

Deep down you know that you want nothing more than peace and a deeply satisfying relationship with yourself, the world, and your partner.

To you, it looks as if everyone else has what you want. Your sister has it, the neighbor has it — they all have it — happiness, love, joy, and the right guy. Or so it appears. After all, what happened to you didn't happen to her (you think).

I honor your courage to step up and say: "I don't have what I want, and I am not feeling my best all the time. I have pain. I can't trust. I never feel safe." Not many people admit that they are in pain, that their hearts are broken. You did. That is mighty.

But where do you go from here?

How can you go from feeling vulnerable, because you are looking the beast right in the eye, to living the life that you want to live? The life that seemingly all those other women have?

This is what *Blossom* is about.

I have been the girl and the woman who compared herself to everything and everyone. For most of my life, I was feeling like my life was wasted, because I had experienced sexual trauma as a child and in my teenage years. My grandfather molested me from the ages of three to seven and my mom's boyfriend beginning at age eleven to thirteen. No matter how hard I tried, I just couldn't "get over it."

I always felt like I was damaged, like I had a bad life, and was somehow cursed by the traumatizing events. Everyone else had more luck in love and life than me. Everyone but me could be happy.

But deep down I knew something better was waiting for me; deep down I had an intense longing to find the love of my life, "the One" who would bring complete fulfillment.

I knew conceptually that if others could get there, I could, too.

What about you? It might feel to you right now as if the world has come to an end. It might feel to you as if things never change and never get better. You might feel very tired about the situation with your partner or about not having a partner. It might feel like you just had a great relationship and now it's gone again. Whatever the case may be, you are finished waiting for things to change and ready to make the change yourself.

This is probably why *Blossom* spoke to you.

You are most likely ready to live a full life, but you just don't quite know how. You know that you are ready to heal and to integrate your traumatic experiences from the past, so they don't keep running your life now.

There is no single path to accomplishing that.

My intention with *Blossom* is to share as much as I can about what it took for me and many of my clients to move from feeling miserable, broken, and lonely to enjoying life and love, feeling safe, and experiencing intimacy with a lover. Living the dream of a "normal" life.

You are very courageous. You are very courageous because you are about to go on a deeply enlightening and freeing journey, but it is new territory and uncharted land. You are taking a leap, so to speak, going where you haven't dared to go before, and you don't know what awaits.

All I can say is, it is never what you think.

I have held the intention and hope for a long time that whatever I had to go through and whatever wisdom I was able to gather along the way might one day be of benefit to others. Now I know that because of the work I have done as a Humanistic Psychotherapist with other women, it will, indeed, help you if you read and take the actions I suggest along the 7-Step Blossom Journey.

Blossom is my story. It is also the story of many women around the globe. I want it to be yours. I want to see you soar and flower. I want to see you flower and fly with an open heart in true love, deep intimacy, freedom, and wholeness.

I am a dreamer and often feel like I should have been born into a different place. I feel like I remember another world – I remember a different life, a different Earth. The place that I remember coming from was drenched in harmony. There was no need for anger, pain or destruction. People were kind and tender, and displayed their open hearts. Men were soft, yet strong, and women were strong, yet soft. There was a sense of balance between the genders and not war. A world where women could be truly feminine and men could be truly masculine.

I am dreaming of that world becoming a reality.

The conclusion I have come to, of what I must do to make this dream place happen here on earth (and I do believe it is possible), is that I must first end the war within myself. And second, I must be able to live peacefully in a relationship with a man by my side.

If you are like me and you remember that peaceful place, too, then do the work of the Blossom Journey and bring it forth with me.

When I started with my own Blossom Journey, I was five months pregnant with my second child, a boy. My first child was a girl. I didn't want to project all my anger and hatred towards men onto my son or model that behavior for my daughter. I also didn't want to end up raising them by myself. I wanted to be a whole and integrated woman, so I could raise my children to become whole and integrated people. I knew that if I was healed, they could grow into adults connected to their heart and not afraid to let all of their actions be expressions of love. I wanted to be fully aligned with my essential being, with my authentic self, to live my life in fullness and wholeness, able to express all my feminine gifts. I knew without a shadow of a doubt that for me, my absolute bliss would come from experiencing my wholeness through the mirror of my true partner. Some call that partner their *soul mate*, others refer to that person as "the One."

Some personal growth paths promote the idea that you must give all the love you need to yourself first, and give up the false hope of meeting and sharing life with another until you do. But I believe that each and every one of us is meant to experience the deepest love possible for human beings through an embodied physical union with another.

Sex and intimacy are a big part of learning to ultimately surrender ones' self to love. I wanted to feel so safe that I would trust my lover more than I trusted myself, to take me open to God and love. I wanted to allow myself to feel and receive my lover's love.

When I started my Blossom Journey, the driving question became, *how can I heal my heart, so I can fully trust another?* The answer that came was this: I had to stop the drama and dysfunction, and step up to creating the dream. There was no other way. So I did. That's how *Blossom* was born.

I am practicing everything I am teaching you, right here and right now, in my life. The journey never really ends. But it does get better and better.

It is my deepest wish that *Blossom* may inspire and support you in starting to write the story of your life, rather than having it written for you. I want you to be able to write a happy and love-filled ending (a never-*really*-ending, ending) to your life. May you blossom through the journey I offer, coming into your own as a beautiful, wild, soft, courageous, strong, gentle, and whole woman.

With deep love and appreciation for all that you are,

Carolin

Introduction

There are rare moments in life when you might meet a woman who touches you in a very special and deep way. She seems at peace with who she is. She radiates beauty and ease. She seems to know the key to her own power, and happiness. She seems so open and accessible, she seems to have it all. But most of all, she is the woman you know you want to be, and that's why she is touching you so deeply.

When you see her with her partner, you can see the deep heart-to-heart connection between them, and you might feel jealous, because you feel that should have been you. When you see her in public, everything is enriched by her smile, her presence, and her being. She is a gift to everyone she meets. You want to be a gift like her. You want to be her.

If you are like me, you've probably wondered, *What is this woman's secret? How has she been able to preserve her heart's innocence and beauty and radiate it so brightly?*

Or perhaps you thought to yourself, *Well, it's easy to be her—she probably never got hurt like me.*

But what if she *did* get hurt. What if she went through similar challenges as you and I? What if she did and was able to rediscover her light and feel safe to let it shine in the world?

What if?

I lived with that *what if* for quite a while. I spent half of my life on finding "her" secret, finding a way to heal my own broken heart and soul. In my quest, I became a Naturopathic Doctor and Humanistic Psychotherapist in my native country, Germany. I spent four years in intensive training to learn what people need to heal. But as it turned out, going to school wasn't enough.

I kept looking for a way, searching and searching until my marriage almost fell apart. I came to the moment when I knew it was now or never. I knew I had to find some answers soon or else my whole dream would implode. The dream of having a happy family and sharing life with my beloved would be gone forever.

I was down on my knees for many, many nights, begging the universe and God to help me. It was through all of these experiences that *Blossom* was born. It came partly because of my professional background but mostly because of my openness to receiving the puzzle pieces I needed to heal. *Blossom* shares with you the *7-Step Journey* that I took to wholeness. And not just me, but women around the world have experienced their very own Blossom Journey as private clients or in my therapeutic groups.

But before you begin on your journey and dive into full "healing yourself" mode, I want to introduce you to how *Blossom* is structured and why this specific structure was chosen.

Blossom is structured into two parts.

Part I is Blossom—My Story. Part II is Blossom—The 7-Step Journey. The reason I am focusing on my own story in Part I is because I have found that we learn new things best from listening to stories. My story of traveling the Blossom journey contains many new insights and paradigms that are essential for you to become familiar with before you begin on your own journey.

In Part II, Blossom—The 7 Step Journey, you will be guided through each of the seven steps towards healing the trauma from your childhood sexual experiences, spending one week on each step. Part II is structured like a workbook, offering lessons and exercises for each day of the seven weeks, along with specific tools for you to use on your healing journey. You will need a journal or notebook for you to write in, as many of the exercises invite you to reflect and write. You will also need Internet access to go online and download occasional guided meditations and other materials.

Are you ready to begin? Hopefully, my story will inspire, support, and show you that there is so much more to healing than you ever imagined...

PART I

Blossom

MY STORY

My Story

This is a story about a girl. An ordinary girl. A girl like you and me, or like you and I once were. A girl who thought she had a bright and shiny future ahead of her. An extraordinary girl that nobody saw, not even herself.

This is a story about a girl who is a woman now, and on her journey to womanhood, went through many trials and tribulations. A woman who longed to meet God (or whatever you call the higher force that governs the universe), longed to have love and intimacy.

It is also about the emptiness she felt, because she never seemed to find what she was searching for. Instead, she sought comfort by eating huge amounts of food, sometimes up to forty pounds worth in a single day, and then purging herself from all she had consumed.

She was never *really* comforted. The food just filled her up and got rid of the pain, at least for a while.

This is also the story of a woman (me) who turned herself inside out and rescued that young girl, so that together they could have a bright future and create a life worth living. It is a story about a woman's victory over primal programming and her liberation from self-defeat.

It is a story about you as well, about freeing yourself from the isolation of your heart that was created along the way.

This story is about the journey to make peace with being born in a woman's body. It's about finding peace in being soft and round and vulnerable inside, and realizing just how strong you are because of it.

It's a story about love. It's about finally finding "the One." The One we all have been searching for since the first fairy tale introduced the concept. It is a story about arrival.

It is my story, but it is your story, too. It is the story of all women.

This story has a happy ending, which is why I am sharing it.

MY OWN LIFE BEGINS

In 1975, my parents got married and merrily set out to create their happy life. What neither of them realized was that they each came with a whole lot of baggage from their past. They unconsciously "saw" in each other the way out.

For my mother, it was the way out of an abusive home with an alcoholic father and a non-protective mother. For my dad, because his mom had left him at age six, it was wanting love and family so much that he latched on the minute he saw something that possibly looked like it.

Needless to say, my mom couldn't make up for my dad's not having a mother, and my dad couldn't compensate for all the scars my mom was carrying.

And then came me. The first born, the savior, destined to make my mom feel happy and my dad feel safe.

My first memory of my earthly arrival was one of glorious hope and deepest disappointment. The hope was that I would make this woman, my mother, happy. I remember being *in utero*, ready to be born, but when I started down the birth canal, I realized that I couldn't make her happy. I felt I had failed in my mission. I can almost remember thinking, *If I can't make her happy, what's the point of being born?*

And so, I tried to stop my birth. My mom was given drugs to make the birth progress. Her being drugged at my birth made me feel even more disconnected then I already felt.

Very few people talk about things like this. People are afraid of this subject, because they would have to rethink the way the birth process is done, especially here in the U.S. Very few people are aware of the fact that whatever happens to you *in utero* and around your birth has a very profound impact on how you lead your life.

Birth—1 hour, 5 hours or 20, no matter how long it takes— is a short time compared to the rest of your life, yet I dare say it is one of the most crucial and defining moments in life. I could go off on an entire tangent here, talking about the birthing system and the dehumanization of the most sacred process (it makes me really, *really* mad). But I will not, since this is not a book about birth.

Let me just mention this. If I had only five minutes in front of the United Nations to give the most important speech of my life, this is what I would say: *Get the men out of the birthing business and let the women and the children do their thing. Be gentle with the baby, greet it in a friendly manner in dimmed light, and never ever separate this new life from his or her mother's or father's warm skin in the first hours, days or even weeks. If you only did this, world peace would increase to 100%, I am sure!*

There you have it. I am very passionate about the connection between mother and child.

I left off where my own birth had come to a halt. Ultimately, though, I was born that same day. They finally pulled me out.

The circumstances of my birth, from the outside, looked perfect. I was a planned baby, very much wished for and well-taken care of. My dad even painted a mural of a farm on the ceiling of our Renault van, so I had something pleasant to look at on the way home from the hospital.

Back in those days, children weren't strapped in car seats but transported in wicker carriers called Moses baskets. It was towards the end of the '70s, June 30, 1978. The hippies had freed a lot of people with their lifestyle, and music of the Beatles, Stones and Cream was blasting everywhere. Brown and orange was the favored color combination and bellbottoms, *real* bellbottoms, were a must-have. The walls of my nursery were orange and my furniture was brown. Oh, and batik was big. I had a handmade lion hamper, a handmade baby blanket, a handmade changing table, a handmade nightgown, a handmade stuffed animal, and a handmade mobile hanging over my bed.

I basically had a handmade everything, and that right there pretty much describes my mother at the time. She was a craftwork and gymnastics elementary school teacher in an orange-brown leotard, and a perfect housewife in her spare time.

The day I was born was the happiest day of my parent's life. I was wanted, expected and loved. We lived in a very rural part of Germany, 30 miles from any city, on top of a big hill. Surrounded by grapes. On the top of that hill were six houses, each with four apartments, and a big old ranch. On the ranch, the government had parked juvenile criminals to keep them away from the rest of the world and try to better them.

My dad had chosen to be one of the heroes to undertake such a fine mission. He was, and still is, a special education teacher. He lives by the conviction that every human being, no matter how bad his actions might appear, has a good heart underneath it all. First he fought with his students, and then he brought his guitar to the class.

We lived in one of the 24 apartments, in one of the six houses that were provided for all the people who worked with these young outlaws. And guess who became my sandbox friends? Yup, all of these "criminals". Maybe not all of them, but at least some.

They were good to me, though. They taught me how to throw a knife and survive alone in the wilderness, and I couldn't find anything wrong with that. To me they were good people who had gotten off to a bad start in life. I felt their pain.

I wasn't the only kid in my family. When I was two, my parents had my brother and three years later, my sister. For a while we were one, big, happy family.

Early on in life though, I started questioning the norm, the way things are done. I began to question reality- was something real simply because you could see it, hear it, smell or feel it? First and foremost, I questioned the way I thought about things and how I thought things should be in life.

Life is a mystery. Period. To this day I haven't figured it out.

The only difference between then and now is that *now* it doesn't drive me to insanity anymore. It doesn't make me close my heart and retreat in fear.

When I look at people and the world around me, I do see a lot of closed-down emotions and a lot of fear. It's understandable that the world and most people seem that way. If you think about it, you don't really ever know what's going to come. You are never going to know for certain that you will see another morning, smell another rose, taste another yummy French kiss, send your kids off to school in the morning, or do the things you have always wanted to do but keep putting off.

That's pretty scary. It used to be for me at least. The truth is that the only thing you can really ever know for sure is that you were created from your father's seed and your mother's egg, that you were birthed by your mother, and that you are going to die one day.

The time in between, the time you call your life, you get to fill, to design, to experience and to live. This feels like a huge responsibility. It feels so huge that it overwhelms almost every human being I have encountered in my life, when they allow themselves to stop and think about it.

Looking back, most of my conscious memories have to do with me and my siblings playing outside, far away from home, far away from civilization. We were hunters and cavemen, explorers and farmers, bakers and chefs, and anything else we could imagine.

Yes, much of my early abuse, the abuse by my grandfather from the time I was three until I was seven, happened during this time. But I had no memory of it until I turned 30, when I explored my past through deep therapy. I really had thought I had a golden childhood up until then. To my conscious recollection, life started to get miserable when I turned eleven.

DEPARTURE FROM CHILDHOOD

Shortly after I turned eleven, things started to change. I felt like I was suddenly being thrown out of paradise. My parents divorced, and a cascade of other "bad things" started to happen, including my mom's boyfriend sexually molesting me. The worst thing was my fear and worry for my little sister, because I didn't want what was happening to me to happen to her.

I lived in constant terror for a couple of years, until finally, one day when my mom's boyfriend came on to me again in an attempt to sleep with me, I somehow got charged with superpowers and freed myself to run away. After that, I couldn't stand being in his presence anymore. Meanwhile, my mom had no clue. So I stopped cleaning up his dishes, started to ignore him, and generally left enough hints for my mom to give her cause to worry.

Not long after this, my mom confronted me about my change in attitude and "rude" behavior towards her boyfriend. That's when I told her that he had repeatedly tried to sleep with me.

Sadly, my mom kind of put it all on me.

He stayed. I left. I moved in with my dad. My heart was broken.

My mother's decision to "side" with him sealed the deal on our disconnection. Today, I know and understand that back then she felt like she wouldn't survive without him, and she probably wouldn't have. But for me, being young and still needing my parents very much, I came to the conclusion that nobody cared about me. God didn't exist, because if He did, how could He let all these bad things happen to me? Needless to say, I was in a lot of despair.

I began to play a game with myself. I had made myself motivational cards for 30 days. My goal was to give myself one card every day as a reward for not eating. The more cards I collected, the more compelling it became.

The 30 days turned into 10 years.

I had found my super powers; I could do what nobody else could. I could control and discipline myself to not eat, or to eat very little for many days. Nothing could hurt me any longer.

Unfortunately though, I grew colder and colder inside. Nothing was fun anymore, and life was only a struggle. I was obsessed with my weight and my body. I was deeply depressed. I was caught in a perpetual spiral that was torturing me day and night. Whenever I walked by a window, I had to look at my body in order to see how "fat" I was. Every woman I came across, I compared myself to, and always lost the competition.

I am too fat. I am too fat. I am too fat. It never stopped. At the time, I weighed 100 pounds and stood 5 feet, 5 inches tall.

My life turned into a prison. I was trapped by time and thoughts. From the moment I opened my eyes in the morning I wished for evening, when I would finally allow myself to eat.

Most people around me didn't notice anything; I was skinny but didn't look sick. I had become a master of deception. Anorexia had turned into Bulimia. I had no hope of ever making it past the 30-year mark and was resigned to live the rest of my life in deep depression and loneliness.

My "Wake Up" Moment

Then, 14 years ago, I had what I call my "toilet-floor wake up moment". It happened in the bathroom as I purged myself from over-eating once again, but this time I realized something: if I continued to do what I was doing, there would be no husband, no kids, no happiness, no joy, no love or intimate connection with "the One" in my life.

It was at that moment of waking up that my journey to healing began.

Since then, I have completely healed from the eating disorders, grown beyond co-dependent relationships, the kind where I lost myself completely, thinking it was love. I have also moved beyond the belief that I had to be "my own man," thinking that I had to be totally self-sufficient, not needing anyone else, if I wanted to be considered a success in life.

My Grail

It was right after my wake up moment that I first encountered Family Constellations, the process I now use with my clients in my own practice. Family Constellation work is very well known in Germany, but here in the U.S. and the rest of the world it is less well known. I have my theory on why that is.

The Germans as a people went through hell and back under Hitler. Some of them became the worst human beings possible, but still they continued on to reproduce and live their lives. All of those who came after the war couldn't fathom what their countrymen, as a people, had done. Some went into complete denial about being German, others tried to justify what had happened, but all of them shared the burden that was almost too heavy to carry.

Today, because of the Second World War, the Germans as a people, and Germany as a country, try to stand for absolute peace and fairness in the world. This transformation was brought forth by the generations after World War II. The generation following the war focused a great deal of energy on healing the wound. They worked hard to establish peace, to return from hell, and to become a good people again. Family Constellations is one of the therapeutic processes that greatly supported that transformation.

I always thought that I didn't feel German because I was just so ashamed for what the Germans did during WWII. As I found out later, this feeling had a very different cause: my mom, though German, was actually born in Serbia.

Serbia had been good to her family, providing them with an abundance of food, joy, love, and laughter. In Serbia, where my mother, grandmother and great-grandmother are from, people used to dance like devils, eat joyously, celebrate frequently, and generally just loved life. Then the war came, and within a few hours, all of that was gone. The houses. The pastures. The laughter and the lives.

My mom wasn't even two years old when she had to leave her motherland, Serbia. Upon arriving in Germany, she was separated from her parents who each individually went into a different refugee camp —one for males, one for females —certainly not a place for a child. This was back in 1955, when my grandparents were still very young.

My mom went to live with her aunt and uncle for over a year. These relatives, who'd arrived back in Germany before her parents did, provided her with good care. But still, uncle and aunt couldn't replace mama and papa and the motherland. She went into silence and never spoke a single word during the time she was with them

Through the Family Constellations work, I learned much about my mother and the nature of her pain. For example, when I was in my mother's womb, a big part of her was still in silence and disconnected from life, so as not to feel the pain of her loss or the pain her family had suffered. Knowing all of this about my own family made me bow in humility.

Family Constellations work brought all this to light, and helped me realize how much pain I was carrying from both my mother and our whole family. It made me understand so many things about myself, including why my relationships were so complicated. Ultimately, it helped me heal, because as I now know, anything that is brought to light can be transformed.

In Part Two of the *"Blossom Journey"*, you will learn about Family Constellations in depth, as well as the insights I have gained from leading so many people through the Constellation process.

At this point, I am hoping to inspire you to start digging, to start bringing to light all that makes up who you are. That's my motivation behind sharing my story, and all that I have found out about my roots. I want you to get curious about yours. It will make a huge difference in all of your relationships, and most importantly, the one you have with yourself.

Today, whenever I meet someone, I am very aware of all that they carry. We can so quickly form judgments about others, but now I catch myself, and at the same time remind myself, of all the lives that have been lived and have contributed to whomever I see, and it leaves me in awe and wonder.

This book is about love and connection. Nothing connects you more to another human being than compassion. As soon as you know someone's whole story, you can't help but feel compassionate towards that person.

The same holds true for you. *What's wrong with me?* is a question that you might have asked yourself often. Nothing is wrong with you, just look at your story the way I will teach you to do in this book. Look through your ancestral eyes. In doing so, you will become illuminated as to the multifaceted baggage, both "good" and "bad", that you have inherited.

TRUE BEGINNINGS

One morning as I sat down to write, I realized that to help you understand my story and see your own in a different light, I had to start with my parents' birth, because their lives and early experiences influenced so much of who I am. Then it occurred to me that my parents' lives were defined by the lives of *their* parents. And then I knew that my grandparents wouldn't be who they were without the impact that *their* parents' lives had on them.

Soon I realized that this could be endless, and that maybe I had better start my life story with Adam and Eve!

Of course, there is no way for me to know any specifics about Eve's life, but I do feel deep in my bones that I still carry the scars and beliefs that were implanted in our first mother. I kept asking myself how my life today is influenced by Adam and Eve's existence. Whether they really lived or not doesn't matter so much to me, because society behaves as if they had, and that is what counts.

After sitting with this question and pondering it for a while, just long enough for my tea to cool down, I realized that my life is indeed impacted by the two of them. Not just a little bit, as in several million years of diluted influence, but in a very big way.

It seems to work like a homeopathic remedy. When a homeopathic remedy is formulated, the extract from the original substance—for example, the herb *arnica*—gets diluted many, many times, and then that dilution gets diluted many, many more times again, until you can't even measure any arnica is in the dilution anymore. But when people put the homeopathic remedy arnica on a bruise, almost immediately the bruise visibly goes away.

That's how I feel it is in terms of Adam and Eve. If you were to look at my genes or cells, or anything else you could measure in my body, you wouldn't find a trace of Adam and Eve. But if you look at my life, or if I look at your life, the impact of our first parents is clear to see.

Quantum physics deals a lot with this phenomenon, exploring the infinite sub-atomic world that cannot yet be directly measured, except by its impact upon the world. Quantum physics points to something being at work that is much grander than we can perceive. This is the same point I am making.

Here is what I see as the impact on us today that stems from Adam and Eve: Eve was held responsible for giving Adam the apple and making him eat from it, and the rather severe consequence was no less than expulsion from the Garden of Eden. Ever since that supposedly happened, ever since that moment, men have been mad at women and have used their superior strength to overpower the "weaker sex."

But there is another meaning to the story. The esoteric, the mystic meaning of the event—and in my opinion the true story—is that all Eve did was help Adam to become conscious of himself, enabling him (and the human race) to live a life in which we have the ability to become free and make free choices.

Eve enabled us to make the choice to become love incarnated in human form, and thus experience our highest potential and joy on earth. She made it possible for you and me to see ourselves as separate individuals.

It is nice to be one in consciousness like a little baby, but as a little baby, you are not conscious of yourself yet, so you are limited in terms of earthly survival. In order to really make the most of your earthly experience, you have no choice but to be conscious of yourself.

In other words, this means that Eve enabled us to free ourselves from subconscious patterns by becoming self-aware, and thus not living on "auto-pilot" anymore, but instead to consciously co-create.

And the guys are mad at her—and all women—for *that?*

The only explanation I can offer for this is that so far, very few men and women truly get the gift that lies within personal freedom and consciousness. But a lot of women I talk to get that they have been tossed out of paradise so they can find their way back and create their paradise in this lifetime on earth.

I believe that you know that both Hell and Paradise are internal states. You've probably done enough work on yourself to figure this out already. But so many others don't know this, and they don't pick up books like this. They stay seated in front of the TV and blame the government or their spouse or their parents for the hell they are living in. As if that Hell were something outside of them, something they had no causal connection to.

But back to the story of Adam and Eve. That's when and where the whole unfairness between men and women began. Eve freed us and she gave us the greatest gift of humanity, yet she was blamed for bringing the original, primal sin upon us.

How about that?

Because of this misunderstanding or misinterpretation, humanity didn't receive Eve's gift. Women, up until now, were regarded as minor humans, needing to be kept under control, needing to pay for the bad thing "she" did, needing to be dominated, so it doesn't ever get too inconvenient for the guys again. All that Eve did was open Adam's eyes to the fact that we are born and we die, and what we do in between is up to us.

It's actually pretty cool when you get it, but as I said earlier, when you stay caught up in "blame mode," it's understandable that you would be mad at the person who you think got you into that predicament.

The reason why I am taking this detour regarding Eve is because being born in a woman's body, as you may have discovered, automatically makes you a sinner, and you have to give penance all your life. Or so it seems.

And that stinks!

Life stinks, or better said, *sucks,* for girls. At least that was what I was feeling most of the time, ever since I can remember. Life's not nice and not fair. Sometimes it feels like there is nothing you can do about it, and then you just wander to the store or the bakery and pull out the credit card and spend another good portion of your life savings on clothes or, in my case, comfort food, or you do something else that isn't good for you...

Because of Eve and this original injustice, I think I was born with a heightened need for fairness and a slight, or rather *tremendous,* outrage at my gender "situation".

I don't know exactly which of my ancestors came after Eve, leading up to the family lineage that I now have direct account of. It really doesn't matter. But I can tell you that there were lots and lots of lives that were lived and people who died so that I could be created.

GOING BACK TO MOVE FORWARD

Here in the Western world, we are so well trained to become independent the moment we breathe that we have forgotten how important our roots are, how they help us to know who we are, and how they guide us through this life.

The reason I am going back in time to tell you my own story is because, as I mentioned before, I made a very profound discovery that was the key to my own healing. For myself, it was necessary to go back as far in my family's history as I could in order to trace the lives that came before mine, lives that contributed to mine, to my journey, and to who I am today.

For most of my life I didn't even know that these people had existed, and I had no interest in ancestry or being connected. I wanted to go out in the world and live my life with lovers and new friends. But my family? Spare me the drama and please leave me alone! I couldn't stand being close. Too much had happened.

I was born a very sensitive child. *Extremely* sensitive. I could feel anything and everything. There was nothing I could do to stop things from going straight to my bones. I wanted to cry often. And I *did* cry often, because I just couldn't control it. The tears would just come out.

People, especially my family, couldn't handle that. Their favorite thing to tell me was, "Well, you are just built too close to the water." I took that to mean there was something wrong with me. I felt wrong for being so sensitive, for being who I was. The only option I saw was to work really hard to make the tears stop, once and forever.

I had to become a grown woman to understand that my sensitivity is my greatest gift and an asset.

This might very well be the same for you.

But back when I was little, the solution or strategy I came up with to not feel anything was to run away from people. I put armor around my heart. I inwardly ran away from my family — ran away from life to hide in a safe cave deep inside the earth, alone all by myself.

Obviously, I didn't really hide beneath the earth, but I did leave my native country Germany. First, I went to live on La Gomera, one of Spain's Canary Islands and later and even further, to California.

This decision made me pretty sad and lonely at times.

Did you make a decision like that, too?

Today, I know without a shadow of a doubt that all the players in my life and all the circumstances in my life were set up for me, so that I would go through exactly what I went through. Including the abuse and abuser.

I did love my grandfather and I still do, even though he is no longer with us. I know he's watching from above and helping me here and there. He knows I am writing this book, and he wants me to help many other women heal. He is okay with me telling my story. He is okay with the world knowing what he did and that on a human level, it was very wrong. But in the greater picture, he was helping me fulfill my purpose here. In a very odd way, what he did to me is helping *you* today.

As for my mom's boyfriend, I did love him, too. Not like a lover, but as a family friend.

He was from Italy and brought with him a lot of passion, *la dolce vita*, a big heart for *la famiglia*, and very *diliciouse* food. He was very young, 23 or so, a lot younger than my mom.

Today, I have no hard feelings towards him, either. I know that he suffered for years for what he had done to me, and the guilt that came with it (and he probably is still living with this burden, since he is a "practicing Catholic"). The fact is, he, too contributed to me helping *you* today.

But I didn't always feel like this.

I had to go into the cave and then pull myself back out in order to learn to appreciate love, life and the light. After all the running away, when I finally couldn't go any further, I discovered that my wholeness, the peace and freedom I was so frantically looking for outside of myself, was lying within me and in my roots all along.

My family is my roots, and I am part of something greater.

Exploring My Roots

My dad has a memory like an elephant—actually, that's not quite accurate. I have a memory like an elephant, but he has a memory like, I don't even know what to call it, ten elephants, a library, the Internet…? He seemed the logical go-to person to get information about my ancestors, and I was right. He remembered lots of stories, and even some facts, about his grandparents and their lives.

Here is a little bit of European history that is mixed with my own personal history (stay with me here you'll see it is important). Back in the mid-1700s, many Germans left the country to serve under Empress Maria Theresia, then ruler of a huge empire that included Austria. Maria Theresia had promised land to all who helped her dig the drainage ditches to rid the land of mosquitoes, and disease. Many in my family went, and years later my great, great grandfather followed them. The country he went to is known today as Serbia, and there he met a woman whose prosperous family owned a hat factory. (I loved finding out about the hat factory, because one of my great loves is hats!)

They married and soon had a daughter. It was the year 1882. That daughter, Emma, was my father's paternal grandmother, my great grandmother.

Emma grew up and married a well-known and respected man in their hometown of Versac, about 40 miles east of Belgrade, the current capital of Serbia. They were well-off and much loved by the community. Their house was always open and music was in the air. They had six children, of whom four boys survived to become adults. (Back then it was common to lose some of your children to diphtheria or other diseases.) The four boys were all very musically gifted. The youngest, Franz Hauser, was my paternal grandfather,.

Life was great. Then World War II came.

My grandfather's three older brothers were drafted, but they all survived the war because they played music so well, and eventually became famous as members of a well-respected quartet It seems that even in wartime, music is loved and used as respite from all that's so ugly.

Franz, my grandfather, was too young to be drafted and so stayed back. His parents sent him to Germany to study music, because they deemed that he would be safe there. Indeed, during his first years in Germany, he had a good life, with many friends and money in his pocket, as his parents were able to send him all the money he needed.

Meanwhile, one morning back home in Serbia, there was a knock on the door, and my beautiful great-grandmother Emma and her beloved husband were given only five minutes to stuff a single pillowcase with whatever they could before being taken to an internment camp, never to return home again.

(Germans living in neighboring countries that didn't join the war "alliance" were heavily persecuted as the enemy after the war was over, the Germans living in the eastern European countries were again persecuted, this time by the Communist regime. Most of my relatives died in that persecution. My great-grandfather died in 1948 in a Communist concentration camp after years of imprisonment and humiliation.)

Years later, Emma was freed through a fortuitous coincidence. One of the guards found out that she was the mother of the then-famous Hauser Quartet, which featured her three sons.

The authorities made a deal with the oldest son; if he would agree to stay with the Communists and not go to Germany, instead teaching them music for the rest of his life, his mother could walk free.

So he did, and she was freed.

Meanwhile, my grandfather Franz was completely alone back in Germany, with a pregnant wife who had counted on his pockets being full of money. That pregnant wife became my own father's mother, a woman who hated her life far too much. Her dream had been to become a famous pianist, and she was very close to fulfilling it, before she had that first child. But after the second and third came, gone was the dream and the opportunity, and all that was left was a woman in rage.

She left her family when my father was still a child of six, and of course it was very hard for him to grow up without a mother. He never really recovered from that shock.

On my mother's side, there were many similar events. They, too, were Germans who had gone east. My mother's paternal grandparents (the parents of the grandfather that abused me) died in the same camp where my father's grandfather, Emma's husband, was kept.

In other words, my mother's father lost both his parents in an internment camp, right before his eyes when he was only 13. He saw them being beaten to death and carted away in an oxcart, naked, to be dropped into a mass grave. No wonder he turned into a raging alcoholic.

Too much pain for one soul to bear.

He met my grandmother, my mother's mother—also known as my beloved *Oma*—several years later, outside of the camp where he was taking care of a local farmer's horses. My grandmother, her mother and her three siblings had also ended up imprisoned in that same camp. They were eventually released to work as slaves in the surrounding countryside, as was my grandfather.

My Oma has told me many stories of her early life. It is unbelievable what she had to go through. Her life also started out very well before everything changed. Her father was a master shoemaker at a fancy shoe factory outside of Apatin, a city 100 miles northwest of Belgrade on the Danube River. They made shoes for British gentlemen. My grandmother still remembers exactly how beautiful their new house was, painted all in white with hand-carved wooden furniture and flowers everywhere. They had a summer and a winter kitchen. A happy childhood on green pastures, with lots of cake and dancing, and joy.

She was 10 years old, and it was 1942.

Her father was drafted that summer. My great-grandmother Theresia was expecting her fourth child. She was 33 years old, and when her husband left, she stayed behind with her three children and the one on the way. She didn't know when or if she'd ever see her husband again.

He came back one more time to see the baby. My grandmother remembers him crying so much when he had to leave again, because he wanted to stay with his family, he didn't want to go back to war. But he didn't have a choice. The baby died shortly after he left, nobody knows why. Then the news of his death arrived. Again, there were knocks on the door. Gun to the chest, pack up your belongings. Five minutes.

Theresia, my great-grandmother, turned from a woman who had it all to a woman who lost her baby, her husband, and all her belongings in just three short months. My grandmother grew up very quickly that summer. She had to. My great-grandmother never came out of her shock and lived the rest of her life in deep depression. My Oma became mother for her two younger siblings.

When my great grandmother Theresia was still alive, she seemed like a grumpy old lady to me. Back then, I didn't know her story, I was too little. Now that I know what happened, I am so sorry that I never took the time to sit with her and hold her hand.

My grandmother and her siblings somehow survived 10 years of prison camp. Winters without firewood, shoes, or food. Slaving, escaping, being captured again, being punished, abused, and almost raped many times. All before the age of 21.

Knowing what I know today, I can't deny that there is a connection between my Oma starving and being in a prison camp from when she was 11 until she turned 21, and me imprisoning and starving myself for the same period of my life. It's as if my soul had wanted to take her pain and say, *See Oma, I am doing this for you, I am standing by your side.*

To make a long story short, out of my eight great-grandparents, only four survived the war, and only one of them ever smiled again. All of them were people just like you and me who went about their lives, took care of their children, and made sure that life continued. They were good people, they were brave people.

They are my people, and I have inherited their strengths.

What I have given you in the past few pages is a lot. I know. A lot of grief, but also a lot of life that wants to continue moving forward.

I am guessing a lot of suffering has happened in your family, too. I am guessing this because I have never encountered anyone in my practice that didn't nod in agreement when I started talking about how we inherit so much from our ancestors.

Breathe and let the sadness be if it wants to come.

And just so you know, my family and I are doing well. Really, *really* well.

And yours can be, too.

Today, I am extremely grateful for the insights into the interwoven pattern of my life that my work as a Humanistic Psychotherapist and Family Constellations facilitator is allowing me to have. Ten years ago, this would have been hard to believe, since it seemed like my family, especially my parents, were the ones causing me all my anguish.

Being a parent is a sacrifice on many levels, giving up a lot of what you like to do. But I think that the greatest gift a parent gives to his or her child is being the one who seems to be the one causing all the pain. It takes a lot to be willing to be that mirror to another soul, in which this other soul chooses to see herself, and it almost always ends up with the child resisting this reflection, running away from it, and fighting against it.

That's what I did, and maybe that's what you are doing, too.

Later on in life, a lover can assume this role of parental mirror for you, but they can always choose to opt out. Your parents never can. They are in it with you for good.

The great news is that we are living in times where it is possible for us to bring peace not only to the generations that came before us, but to our own family and to our own hearts.

Are you ready for the journey?

Turn the page and let your own Blossom Journey begin.

PART II

Blossom

Your 7-Step Journey For Healing Childhood Sexual Abuse and Creating Your Dream Life!

Prologue to Part II

Let's get to work, shall we?

Before we start buckling up and tying our shoelaces, let's make sure we have everything we need to succeed on this journey. The first thing you do before going on any journey is to plan and educate yourself. You plan how long it will take, where you will start, where you will rest and when, and when you want to arrive. In addition to that, you also find out what conditions to expect and what equipment to bring. It's no different with the Blossom Journey.

Here is the plan that will get you to your destination:

Look at the Blossom Journey as you would a new exercise regimen. As with learning any new skill, you cannot get the results you are looking for by merely reading through the information and the exercises. If you want to get into better shape you don't stop exercising all of a sudden just because you know the exercises.

It's the same here. For visible results, ongoing practice is required. You might choose to read the entire seven steps of the Blossom Journey once through and then go back and do the exercises. Or you might choose to carve out the time right now and commit to spending 20-45 minutes a day, preferably in the morning, with this book. If you do the Blossom Journey as written and do one lesson of each step per day, it will take you seven weeks to complete.

If this seems like a huge commitment to you right now, consider how much time it will take to care for your ideal life and relationship on an ongoing basis, and consider your commitment as practice time for the "real deal." Some people like to work in a less linear way, so if this is you, read through one week at a time and then do one exercise one day and three exercises the next. Some people will just go at their own pace and do an exercise here and there, and complete the Journey in six months or even a year.

It's important to keep in mind that there is no right or wrong way of going through this Journey. Life isn't about perfection and nor is this journey; it's about fully participating and growing. You want to make sure that you move forward, or else you will not arrive at your planned destination.

Here is an overview of the territory that lies ahead. As if by magic, the word *Blossom* consists of seven letters, each one representing the seven individual steps for each week of the journey. You can look at these steps like guideposts along the way, your landmarks on the treasure map. Before you get into the process itself, let's look at what each letter stands for as the theme for each week:

B: *Bring Your Mind on Board*

L: *Land Within Yourself*

O: *Open to Your Intuition*

S: *See with Eyes of Truth*

S: *Stretch Beyond Your Limits*

O: *Own All of Who You Are*

M: *Meet the World and Your Beloved in Wholeness*

Now let's look at what you can expect. The Blossom Journey is about learning how to live with an open heart in any situation, whether you are in a relationship or not.

I do believe that we are all meant to experience love with another. As mentioned before, it's my belief that just loving yourself is not enough. While loving yourself is a good thing, loving *only* yourself and being self-sufficient will never be the fulfillment of your dreams, of your deepest desire for love.

If the right partner hasn't shown up in your life yet, just know it simply means that you still have more work to do. That's what *Blossom* is meant to do, to help you with that work. If you are currently with a partner, but are still longing for more love and intimacy, then the same holds true. That's how it was in my own case.

The truth is, the work in a relationship never ends.

The work that is in front of you might entail leaving your current partner and being alone for a while, or it might not. As you grow, your partner may grow, too. I can assure you that whatever is needed for you to have a deeply fulfilling relationship with your current or future partner and yourself will become apparent.

If you are growing apart from your current partner, just know that it's a natural progression for both of you. Not every relationship is meant to last. How long a relationship lasts is not the true measure of success. The true measure of success for relationships is whether you both learned whatever you needed to learn, and have expanded your capacity for love and peace once that relationship has ended.

After all, is it really a successful relationship just because you stick it out, let it go sour or drag it on forever? Is it a successful relationship when both of you suffer for no good reason other than the fear of failure or loneliness?

Now that you have started to make plans for the duration of your journey and you have gotten a glimpse of the route that lies ahead, and you know some of what to expect, let's make sure you have the right equipment.

EQUIPMENT YOU WILL NEED FOR THE JOURNEY

Get a binder, or use one you already have. Make it special. Decorate it with a picture of you and your beloved, a picture of you enjoying one of your favorite hobbies or pastimes, a clipping from a magazine that represents you in your power, a beautiful flower, whatever represents the best possible outcome of this journey to you.

Next, download the *Blossom Transformation Guide*, a free workbook that will help you do the recommended exercises and also provide pages for you to journal. Go to www.Blossombook.com/guide for the free download. After you have downloaded the guide, print it and insert it into your binder.

Next, get your planner out and pencil in the specific time, each day, when you will commit to spending time with Blossom. Again, choose what works best for you, but make sure it is something you can commit to on a regular basis. I always teach my clients that regularity is key when going through transformation. This is very important. Otherwise, you might get thrown off track by your own unconscious resistance.

Consciously take this time for yourself and make it a sacred ritual. If you have children, make sure you choose times when you will not be interrupted.

Now that you are all packed and ready, there is one last step you have to take before commencing. Any Journeywoman, or Journeyman for that matter, is condemned to fail if he or she doesn't have a firm commitment in their heart. So your first assignment is to make a commitment to your own healing journey.

YOUR FIRST ASSIGNMENT

A commitment to the Blossom Journey is a commitment to love itself, to exploring what true and empowered love *really* is. On page one of the *Blossom Transformation Guide*, you will find the Love Commitment Form, and on it is written the following sentence: *I, _____, hereby commit to love itself.* Fill in your name and sign and date the Form. When you are done, you are officially ready.

Commit to love itself. When you do that, fear abates, and you can make your decisions based on freedom.

Some last words before we "take off". There are many new concepts that you will be introduced to on this journey. Each time you are introduced to a new concept, consider the following two questions:

1. *Do I believe this concept to be true?*

2. *Is there a place in me that agrees with what Blossom is teaching me right now?*

I would never want you to blindly believe anything I say or teach. Everything I teach and share comes from a place of love and a deep wish to support you. Everything I share with you here was vital to my own journey and to the journey of many women I have had the honor of working with. But it is very important that each of the concepts feels right to you. That's why answering these two questions is an essential part of the process.

Blossom is a gentle journey, one that brings all of your different parts along.

Lastly, remember to have fun with all of this! Truly, treat this book as the key that life has given you to help unblock and unlock everything that is holding you back from being in your authentic power and experiencing the deep love, intimacy, joy, ecstasy, closeness, trust and fun with a beloved and in your life.

Week One
Bring Your Mind on Board

This first step and week of the Blossom Journey primarily addresses your mind and mental capacities. The reason for that is simple. When we heal, we journey from the mind into the heart, so the mind is a good place to start.

The mind is the place people are usually the most comfortable. It feels familiar and safe. Being in your mind and making decisions and interactions from that place is what society teaches. Moving out of your heart and into your head is also what happens to you when you depart from childhood and enter into adulthood, but more on that in Week 6.

Journey from Mind into Heart

As mentioned, the Blossom Journey is one from the head to the heart, from thinking your way through life, to feeling and participating fully in it.

While a lot of the work on this journey is aimed at healing your emotional wounds, it is very important to keep your mind engaged and in sync with the healing process. As you may have realized already, your mind's many voices have been the leading contributor to your inability to trust, as well as your inability to have the life and relationships you say you want.

Your mind has a great deal of power over you. You want to make it your friend, so you can use its brilliance to help you in accomplishing our goal. Your mind needs to be able to see and to measure progress. The mind is a wonderful tool, but it shouldn't be your trusted advisor when it comes to love, life, or change.

If you have ever tried to lose weight or start a new exercise regimen, you know how much resistance you encounter. Whenever you start something new, part of you is very scared, because it doesn't know what lies ahead. This scared part is one of the very strong voices in our head.

It is the part that is afraid and would rather keep the status quo, even if it's not a perfect life or even if it is bad (like being in an abusive or co-dependent relationship or being alone), because the life that is known is at least predictable and quantifiable. Change is not quantifiable.

This part of you that is afraid of change is your *wounded inner child*. Most of us don't know that our wounded inner child makes up a big part of our subconscious. This wouldn't be so tragic if the decisions we make in life weren't influenced 80 percent by our subconscious.

In other words, four fifths of your life is guided predominantly by your wounded inner child. It's very powerful. Its goal is to keep you safe—and comfortable. When you try to change, it gives you many different but very good reasons not to change. Those reasons are the resistance you encounter when you want to change.

In Week One, you and all your parts, including your inner wounded child, will be introduced to five core concepts that will help your inner child feel safe. In the next week, we can go a step further and consciously reconnect with this part of you and help it heal.

By thoroughly working through this first week, you lay the foundation for the support of your mind. When you have a clear mental understanding of where you are starting from, and exactly where you are going, the idea of change doesn't seem so unquantifiable and scary anymore to your wounded inner child. It will help your mind and the part of you that doesn't want change to calm down.

LESSON for Day One

GETTING READY FOR CHANGE

On this first day of your Blossom Journey, I ask you to question what you have believed about yourself so far. This will make you question the things that your mind tells you to do, think, or be. One result might be that you stop "lying" to yourself about the state of your wellbeing, about the state of your relationship, or about the way you feel.

This may sound like a harsh beginning, but it is a necessary one. As long as we are thinking thoughts like, *Well, I don't really have a problem, all is good, my relationship will get better one day, he will change someday or I am just not worthy of love, something is wrong with me*, then nothing will change, and you will continue to be unhappy.

Some people spend their entire life that way. You know them as well as I do. I am assuming you don't want to be one of them. Change is a good thing. Intuitively, I sense you know this already.

MELTING THE RESISTANCE

Once you recognize the lies you have been telling yourself, they start to fall away, because you are becoming more and more authentic. When this happens, it will serve as proof to your mind that what you are doing is good for you. Then, your mind will no longer advise you to stop growing.

Once your mind begins to feel safer with the new evolving you, then it will allow you to go deeper. It will, perhaps for the first time in a long time, stop coming up with all kinds of reasons why you shouldn't change. When you begin to open up emotionally, your mind's voices will no longer advise you to run and close down anymore. It will encourage you to stay. When you are honest with yourself, you have a solid base to start from. It gives you a starting point from which you can begin to trust yourself.

When you are able to trust yourself, you can slowly but surely begin to trust someone else, too. As I am sure you know, love, intimacy and living fully can't be experienced without trust.

Being honest with yourself, accepting and seeing the real state of your internal affairs, takes a lot of courage. You have already mustered quite a lot of it simply by picking up this book. Honesty is key to any real growth. Being honest with yourself is the foundation of real growth. Being honest with yourself allows hurting parts to emerge and be seen, allowing transformation and healing. When you stop looking outside and start looking inside, you start to receive the answers you have been waiting for. Inside is where all your answers lie.

EXERCISE

TAKE INVENTORY

All successful journeys begin with making a checklist of what is on board and what is not. Get out your journal and take an inventory about yourself and your growth to this point in life. Spend time with the question: *Are there things in my life that I have not been honest about with myself and others?* If your answer is yes, then write down what those things are. Do not censor yourself. Allow yourself to want it all. Imagine you can have it all.

Lesson
for Day Two

Nobody Out There Can Save You

In what I've referred to as my toilet wake up moment, finding myself once again on a lonely bathroom floor sticking a toothbrush down my throat to gag and vomit the huge amount of food I'd eaten, I realized I wasn't very far from death. My parents kept telling me I'd end up just like Mama Cass, the famous singer from the Mamas and the Pappas who suffered from bulimia and supposedly died choking on food on the bathroom floor. I also realized that up to my own toilet floor moment, I believed that someone "out there"—the therapists, the doctors and the healers—were the experts to rescue me. I had been hoping, praying, even begging, that one of them would figure out what was wrong with me. Then, they could fix me and make me all better.

But what hit me the night of my wake-up call was this: There never, ever would be, or could be, anyone "out there" who would just wave a magic wand and make me healed, make it as if the trauma I'd experienced had never happened.

It was at that moment that I found the courage to heal myself. I knew that I had to be the one to do it, or it would never really happen. It became clear to me that I was the only one who could heal my broken heart.

In your case, it's the same. You are the only one who can heal yourself. There is nobody else who can do it. Only then can you open your heart and feel safe. When you understand this, it enables you to take the firsts steps toward healing. Only then will you finally stop waiting for someone else to heal you.

STOP WAITING

You are being introduced to this concept of no one being "out there" early in your journey, because it will help you to shift from waiting for things to change to taking proactive steps. Being proactive is far better than waiting for someone to come and finally help you, or for your man or partner—or life—to finally change.

Picking up this book and committing to working through it means you are already taking a proactive step. Realizing that you are the only one who can really heal yourself helps you to get from a place where you are the powerless victim to reclaiming your power. You do this by changing what no longer works in your life and in your relationships.

You may have thought, or hoped, that I would be the one saving you. Or maybe this book would be the one that did that for you. But really, both Blossom and I are here to remind you of all the things you already know on some level.

Your soul knows, for sure.

A WORD ON TRADITIONAL THERAPY

I went to a number of analytical therapists for many, many years. The only results were that my parents ended up spending a ton of money on therapy bills.

If you have been seeing a therapist for quite a while, haven't you wondered, deep down, why is it taking so long? Why don't you seem to be getting any closer to healing? Why are you still angry at your man or at men, and why are you still fighting all the time? Why can't you let go during sex or feel connected and close? Why does life seem so hard?

When I was going to therapy, I started wondering and asking all these same questions, too. What I realized, finally, was this: Traditional therapy is only focused on treating or fixing the problem, not on *transforming, integrating, learning from* or *healing* the problem.

Big difference! Putting a band-aid on a gushing wound doesn't make your wound heal, nor does it help new skin to magically grow. In other words, traditional therapy often fails, because it focuses on fixing the symptoms (the gushing wound), but not on supporting the body's own healing powers and healing the cause. It doesn't help us to journey out of our head and into our heart. It stays up there, bringing confusion and giving us a headache!

You are the one who knows how to heal your heart best. You'll see that's true on this journey.

EXERCISE

STOP WAITING

Get out your journal and ask yourself this question: *Am I still hoping that someone out there will help me?* Write honestly.

Or, did you already have your own wake-up moment and realize that there is no one out there to rescue you? If you did, go back in time and find it. Write it down. Remember the thoughts that crossed your mind. They were most likely given to you by grace. Become as conscious of it as possible, so you can reconnect with the energy of the event over and over again. This is what will keep you on the path when times get tough. It will also help you to make this concept a real truth for you, rather than only an abstract mental concept or memory.

LESSON
for Day Three

RESPONSE-ABILITY

Generally, when we hear the word *responsibility*, we think it means a heavy burden, doing things right, the way society expects you to act, etc.

This is not what today's lesson is about. When looking at the word *response-ability*, you can see that it simply means "able to respond." Response-*ability*, meaning your ability to respond to whatever life brings you.

Right now, in the beginning days of our journey together, it is only necessary for you to know that personal response-ability is one of the goals we are working towards. You don't yet have to know how to "do" or "be" it. The goal for today's lesson is to understand what it means to be response-able, and to see where you are, on a scale of 1 to 10, in your ability to respond. Again, it's about being honest with yourself, and about who you are. You might think you are the most loving person in the world, but in all honesty, the reality might be somewhat different.

Let's explore more deeply what it means to be able to respond. For example, does it mean you are able to respond, or answer a question when asked? You might think so, if you take the word literally. However, that's not what I mean. What I do mean is that you are able to be non-reactive when something or someone comes towards you, when things seem to "just happen" to you.

As long as you are trapped by feelings of unworthiness due to your early sexual trauma, your life feels like it is "just" happening to you. Your lover "just" treats you badly and has no respect. Your friends or colleagues are "just" unreliable. Your family "just" doesn't care or weighs you down with guilt. Whatever it might be, it seems that others are the ones who are causing you all the pain. I call that state of mind "victim mentality". You feel like a victim, because you have been a victim early on, and that's just how you have come to relate to life.

You probably have heard it said that you are the creator of your own life, your own circumstances. Yet it seems like that can't be true. If it were true, why would you attract so much drama and trauma to yourself? No one would want that, right? Nevertheless, I am daring to say that we all do.

When they first come to me, most of my clients have a case of the "poor me's," another name for victim mentality. When someone has the poor me's, they perceive life as happening to them without seeing how they are contributing to it.

Being in victim mentality is a sign that a person is not yet able to respond, be response-able, to life. If this is you, be honest with yourself about it and please do forgive me for being so blunt. I needed someone to be blunt with me, because I was stuck in thinking "poor me" all the time. The problem is that the poor me thinking creates new drama, trauma and unhappiness.

Response–ability means that you are able to pause, reflect and get clear on what's best for you and for everyone involved. Being response-able means that you are able to make a choice out of love, rather than out of fear or old programming. It means you are able to stop the drama. In contrast, when you are reactive, your heart is closing down. When your heart is closed down, you can't feel love. A closed heart causes you to do un-loving things. Then, guess what? Other people do unloving things back. If you react a lot, you are in a state of closed heart a lot. Your closed heart is the cause of most of the pain you are feeling. It is what blocks you from experiencing feelings of love, intimacy, and power.

Chances are, if it hurts us, it hurts someone else, too. So in order for us to experience more love and intimacy, the main thing we need to do is to open our heart, and keep it open. I know this might sound not very "psychological". It might seem too simple and possibly too spiritual. But it is the truth.

Keeping your heart open is the key.

I am giving you the key here. In order for you to experience intimacy and empowerment, and to have the relationship you say you want, you need to keep your heart open.

In order to start to open your heart, you need to first realize it is *you* who is closing it down. And so it is your own commitment to growing your ability to respond that will allow you to open your heart.

When you realize that you are really the one that is closing your heart, you realize that you are the one who can learn to open it and therefore respond to life. I know that keeping your heart open at all times is far easier said than done. Only saints and angels can do it all the time. If it was so easy, we wouldn't need to read a book about it, nor would we need to continually practice and practice, and then practice some more.

REACTIVE VS. RESPONSIVE

Let me give you an example scenario of *reactive* vs. *responsive* behavior. It's one plucked right out of real life, a common scenario that my clients describe when they come to me for help:

A woman has a conflict with her lover because she has to work all week, and she only has time to see him at a certain time and date. She wants him to commit, to promise to spend that time with her. But for his own reasons, he can't. She gets angry and feels like he does not love her. She thinks that if she were his first priority, he would cancel everything and just commit. She is very upset and is reacting to what she sees as his failure to commit, his failure to fully love her.

Her first impulse is to blame him for how she is feeling. She might call him an asshole or worse, even get physical. She might think thoughts like, *He's just in it for the sex,* or *stupid bastard, he doesn't deserve a good woman like me.* The two of them get into a fight and then he leaves because he doesn't want to deal with her. Almost immediately, she regrets her outburst but it is too late; he is now pushed away. She tries to make herself feel better, so she goes out to buy an expensive handbag, shoes, lingerie—you name it—or she lights a cigarette, pours a drink, or stuffs herself with food.

Then she comes to me and asks how she can stop the pain and win him back.

The above scenario illustrates my client is in a *reactive* state. She is unable to respond appropriately to the situation. Her wounds have been triggered, and she doesn't know how to stop the pain, other than fighting against it. She is not in control of her emotions. Something else seems to be controlling her, or at least that's how it feels.

She is not able to respond. Even worse, her inability to respond appropriately creates drama and, in extreme cases, new trauma. It's a vicious cycle. If she was able to respond, as opposed to react, she would notice that, because he is not immediately committing, something inside her gets "triggered". This causes her to get angry. If she had learned to respond rather than react, she would contain herself and not lash out. She would let the feelings take their course and she would get to the truth of the matter. Then, once her emotions had calmed down, she would ask herself what Love would say, do or be in that moment.

She might say something like this to her partner: "I understand that you can't commit right away. What I want is to spend time with you, because I love you. When you don't commit, it feels to me like you don't love me. I know that is not the case. I am insecure about love. When I get insecure about your love for me, I close down. Then, I don't feel any love at all.

I become angry with you for causing me pain, though I know you are not the cause of my pain. My old wounds and my closing down are the cause of my pain.

You are serving as a mirror to point them out. By pointing them out unconsciously through your manifestations, I get the chance to become aware and to heal. Thank you for being willing to be in relationship with me, and to help me heal."

That is an example of a responsive state. The ability to respond would have enabled her to process her emotions in a healthy way and communicate in a way that creates *connection* rather than *separation* between her and her partner. Her lover would have felt attracted by her loving and her vulnerability, and would most likely do everything possible to be with her on the date and time she had requested, because he loves her, wants to make her happy, and wants to be in her sweet love.

By responding rather than reacting, she would have gotten just what she wanted. She would have had an experience of love. She would not have gotten angry at him, and it would not have set up the chain of events that occurred once she did become angry.

But not getting angry when your lover happens to trigger an old wound is not so easy. It's the hardest thing to do in love. Yet that's the work that is required to make love last.

It's not something that you can do with your will power alone. I am sure you have tried that many times. You promise yourself to be nice and understanding, and then suddenly, he does something that hurts you so much that you are at his throat once again.

Most of what you will learn and do in the next several weeks will focus on becoming aware of and integrating, the stuff that makes you react. This will help enable you to respond, and to make conscious, rather than reactive, choices out of love. This is where true freedom lies.

The following exercise will help you to get the concept of re-sponse-ability. It will take it out of the conceptual realm and put it into your own experience. By doing this, you will make it real and true for you.

Exercise

How Reactive Are You?

Throughout your day, pay attention to the moments you react. In the evening, write in your journal about your experience. In doing this, you'll be able to see how reactive you are by the number of times you reacted throughout your day. If you found yourself screaming and yelling all day, you've got your work cut out for you!

But that's not necessarily a bad thing. Just by becoming aware of the reality that you are reacting, you are starting to heal. Again, awareness is the first step in healing.

LESSON for Day Four

YOU ARE NOT BROKEN

Frequently, when a woman is a "survivor" of trauma and abuse, she feels broken by the event and often wonders if she can ever feel unbroken. She doubts that she can ever be "fixed." There is a deep sense of wrongness within her because of what has happened to her, and this deeply affects her sense of worthiness and her self-esteem. So many women come to me with the heartbreaking question, *What is wrong with me?* I just want to shake them and wake them up, opening their eyes to the magnificent being that they are. But they don't remember.

When you are first born, nothing is wrong with you. You are an innocent newborn, helpless and totally dependent on whoever takes care of you. In most cases, the caretaker is your mother, God bless her. The only way to convey your needs is through crying. If you are lucky, your caretaker interprets your crying correctly. In that case, your needs get met. More likely, your needs aren't understood. Your caretaker doesn't see your cries as a way of communicating. They are experienced as an annoyance. Back when you and I were little, and even today, many babies weren't seen as equal to adults in their needs. When adults feel helpless and don't know what to do with a baby's cries, they feel annoyance. If our adult caregivers frequently react to our needs with annoyance, eventually, we start to believe that something is wrong with us.

Over time you develop insecurities about yourself. You forget who you really are and what you came here to be and do. At best, you simply adapt. More likely, you go into a kind of psychic hibernation just to survive childhood. The problem with psychic hibernation is that it is a survival mode, not a *thriving* mode. In pure survival mode, or even adaptation mode (which means doing what grownups want you to do, rather than what you really want to do), life isn't much fun at all. It invites predators to take advantage of you. The reason for that is you have basically checked out of your body, and you are no longer present in your life.

Leaving Your Body

For survivors of abuse, parts of the soul and spirit leave the body, going away to some other place and leaving the rest without protection. With each additional trauma, another part checks out, and then the parts that are left behind are exposed to even greater trauma.

I will explain this in more depth in Step Six of the Blossom Journey, where you will learn about "owning yourself," and how the nervous system responds to and deals with trauma. Most importantly, you'll also learn what you can do to heal your own trauma. For now, I just want you to understand that this does happen.

Most of us stay in survival mode and adaptation mode, because we fear being alone and not being accepted by society or our family. The reason why we fear not being accepted by our family is because changing our circumstances would mean doing it differently than the rest of our clan. In ancient times, when we did things differently than our clan, we were left on our own, and that meant very slim chances of survival. The need to belong is so huge.

This is very primal stuff. It's is not a conscious decision you make, it's subconscious.

Because you subconsciously don't want to risk your survival by being cast out from your clan, you do everything the way it was always done. This means you never really get out of your feeling "small and helpless" zone. You think something is wrong with you because, generally, you are not taught that it is natural to have *individual* needs. Feelings like wanting to be you, wanting love and intimacy, having deep desires (such as those sexual in nature), and wanting to have those needs fulfilled, are extinguished.

How Love Got So Confusing

As a young girl, you were probably raised to ignore your own needs and do what everyone else wanted. In that situation, you allowed things to happen to you and to your body that you didn't want. You think it is right because you love the other person, and they are older and must know better than you as to what's good or bad. And since you do love them, you are also sure that they love you, and what they do to you is just another expression of their love.

This is how love got so confusing for you. This is why a lot of my clients are alone and don't have partners; they have decided to be safe, rather than to allow a love that hurts.

It was the same for me. My own early abuse by my grandfather left me extremely confused, because I loved playing with him. I loved him *period*. I was confused because he shifted from being my normal grandpa to being this "other person". When I first remembered the abuse in my early thirties, I expected to feel angry, but I didn't—I just felt so utterly confused.

And of course, when you are confused, you think something is wrong with you.

The reality is that when you are confused, you are simply not clear. You are not clear about love and you doubt your own power. You are not clear that you *are* that love and that power— it is your very essence. You think you are broken, but the truth is you are not. At your core, you are love. At our core, each of us is love. And that is the source of your power.

You came as love into the world. I know this sounds very spiritual and "new age," but just look at any newborn. A newborn is pure love. You were a newborn once, weren't you? So there you go.

Shortly after my toilet wake-up moment, I was introduced to the writings and teachings of Marianne Williamson. One of her famous quotes from *A Return To Love: Reflections on the Principles of A Course in Miracles* struck a deep chord within me:

> "Our deepest fear is not that we are inadequate. Our deepest fear is that we are powerful beyond measure. It is our light, not our darkness, that most frightens us. We ask ourselves, who am I to be brilliant, gorgeous, talented, and fabulous? Actually, who are you not to be? You are a child of God. Your playing small doesn't serve the world. There's nothing enlightened about shrinking so that other people won't feel insecure around you.
>
> "We are all meant to shine, as children do. ... And as we let our own light shine, we unconsciously give other people permission to do the same. As we are liberated from our own fear, our presence automatically liberates others."

This quote helped me a great deal in returning to my path. It shook me to the core and contributed greatly to my transformation. It took me right out of hibernation and back into full living and loving mode. Her words have become my guidepost ever since. I actually have them hanging on my wall. I look at them every day and ask myself: *Am I letting my light shine?*

If you are like me, you have tried many things to fix yourself. Can you see now how all of these approaches were based on the false belief that you are broken and needed fixing? Realizing that you are not broken by the events that happened to you is essential to healing your heart, and keeping it open. I will say this over and over again: Your open heart is your solution to experiencing a safe, peaceful, powerful, and joyful life. Your personality, as well as other parts of you, might feel damaged. But remember that your essence, the being that you really are, can't be damaged. Know that your essence is pure, eternal love.

Finding ways to connect to that eternal part within you and realizing more and more of your essential being while here on earth is, in my opinion, one of the most rewarding aspects that growing and transforming has to offer. Healing your heart really is about embodying the truth about love, about yourself and all other beings.

SCIENTIFIC PRAYER

A tool that I discovered when I first came to the U.S. was the scientific prayer of Science of Mind, a spiritual community and philosophy. Their core belief is that all is God and God is Love.

Therefore, in truth, all there is, is love.

One of the services that they offer is something they call a "prayer hotline," which is a free service where you call a trained practitioner who offers a prayer for you. All you have to do is listen. I used it extensively when I needed to be reminded of my true nature. I still use it today and invite you to do the same. All you have to do is type "science of mind" into a search engine to find a community near you. You can call and tell them you want support in seeing yourself as whole, and they become that support.

EXERCISE

GUIDED PRAYER

Today, I have a gift prepared for you. Go to Blossombook.com/recordings and download the recording of a guided prayer and a guided meditation spoken by my favorite practitioner, Linda Lee. Listen to the guided mediation, and then record your thoughts and feelings in your journal.

LESSON for Day Five

INTEGRATION: WHAT YOU REALLY WANT

In the last lesson, you were introduced to the concept that no one is ever really broken. It's only your perception of your persona that causes you to think you're broken. Today we will look at yet another aspect that contributes to the notion that you are broken and need fixing, the "healing" paradigm.

The concept of "healing" that Westerners use implies that something is broken and needs fixing, that something is wrong with you. The truth that I have found, however, is that as long as you think you need healing, you think of yourself in terms of "broken-ness," and "something's-wrong-with-me"-ness.

To *integrate*, on the other hand, means that you simply digest something you haven't fully digested yet. Digestion happens all day and night long, throughout your entire life. It's a natural and required process for you to be able to live. The same is true for integration. It's a natural process that is required for you to truly grow and evolve.

When trauma happens, we are given a very big bite to digest/integrate. In today's culture we are not given time and understanding to chew this bite up and make it part of us through digestion and metabolism. We are expected to swallow it whole and move on as if nothing had happened. When we do that, we literally carry this big undigested lump in our body and soul. We are constantly reminded of it because it isn't chewed up, it is as if it were laying heavily in our stomach. It bothers us and holds our attention at all times, because it just feels so darn wrong. Just like you feel when you eat something greasy and heavy that your stomach can't handle. It weighs heavily on us.

But the goal isn't that you get back to "the way things were before." By digesting your trauma through integration work, you make it a part of yourself. It becomes a part of you, like your beautiful eyes or your hair. It's just a part of who you are, no longer a disability or hindrance.

By integrating your trauma rather than trying to heal it and make it go away, you allow yourself to truly move forward and become a free woman.

No one talks about this in today's society. Trauma is a taboo. That's why almost no one talks about how to really deal with it.

Thinking in terms of integration will help lift the taboo of trauma and make it a part of life that we all share. I am inviting you to make that shift.

As mentioned, later in Week Six, I will spend more time explaining how integration happens, and specifically, what you can do to integrate and digest your undigested experiences. Again, my intention in these early days of this journey is to introduce you to new concepts, so your mind can get the whole picture and support you in your growth.

From here on in, I will be using the word *integration* rather than the word *healing*.

As for myself, even though some people might refer to me as a healer, and to my work as healing work, I actually see it quite differently.

A Word about Healers

I always get suspicious when people call themselves healers, because to me, being able to support individuals in their growth process requires first and foremost an ability to see them as they are. As discussed earlier, this is seeing someone as whole, not broken, but simply in need of digesting certain things. If I call myself a healer, I am saying I have something you lack, a wholeness that you don't have. It strongly implies that I can do something for you that you can't do for yourself.

The truth is, nobody else can integrate your stuff. Only you can integrate what you need to integrate.

I see myself as someone who teaches by providing tools and processes for integration. I also help facilitate the integration process of individuals, but I am very clear that other than supporting and teaching, there is nothing I can do. My clients have to do their own work. And they are very capable of doing it.

If you stay within the healing paradigm vs. the integration paradigm, you give up some of your own response-ability, because you think someone outside of yourself can do your work for you. No one else can eat or drink and nourish your body for you. No one can nourish your soul but you.

When you give up both the need and the thought that you can get back to the way you were, which is what healing implies, only then are you ready for integration. Integration can occur once you are ready to be where you are with all that you have experienced. At this point, your choices and your reactions are no longer based on the past, but on the present. When you have integrated your "bad" experiences, you are free to make new and healthy choices.

You can know that integration has occurred when things that used to scare you don't scare you any longer. When things that were difficult and upsetting, like being intimate with your man or a man are no longer difficult. When saying *no* when you mean *no*, and *yes* when you mean *yes* is what you naturally do.

You know you have integrated your trauma when you can talk about your story without being upset by it, or feeling like your story determines who you are.

All of the tools and concepts introduced in the Blossom Journey are geared towards helping you achieve integration and freedom from emotional slavery.

Exercise

Recalling Your Integration

Look back at your life and see if you can find moments when you integrated an experience. Find examples in your life that show to your mind and your scared inner two-year-old that you have had "integration" experiences. Write out these integration scenes and "play" them in your mind.

EXAMPLES OF INTEGRATION EXPERIENCES

My client Sherry always felt uneasy when her mom gave her gifts and said, "I love you." She felt like her mom only said it because she wanted something from her. The gifts and words made her feel suffocated. After she learned to allow herself to be with the feeling of suffocation and digest it, things changed. She now can allow herself to feel her mother's love.

Another example comes from my own experience: I was mad at my boyfriend for not calling me, but instead of drinking a glass of wine and getting wasted, I simply sat there and endured the intense feelings in my stomach and the screaming voices in my head. After that, this reaction never happened again, because I had integrated that experience. I did not have to recycle it every time he failed to call, but was free to make another response, one that was more productive in the long run.

LESSON for Day Six

STOP ASKING THE QUESTION: WHY?

Analytical therapy, which was mainly the type of therapy I was sent to during my teenage years, made it seem that if I could figure out all the reasons why things happened to me, I would be healed. I managed to fill hours and hours of time with my therapists, theorizing about the things that happened, that might have caused my pain, my messed up relationships, and my troubled life in general.

But here's the thing: My self-destructive behavior, the binge eating and starvation cycles, the habit of getting involved with the wrong people—none of that went away. There was no increase in my level of happiness or peace. Today I know that the thing that kept me bound to the past was my continual asking of the question, *Why?*

The past never holds the key to wholeness.

You are who you are because you have lived a unique life. In order to get different results out of life from this point on, you have to do things differently. You can only do things differently when you have gained the capacity to respond to life rather than to react.

When you are able to respond to life, you can start looking towards solutions that help you feel more at peace, safer, more joyful. Again, it all boils down to being in touch with your heart, and knowing what you really need and what is good for you. Knowing these things, you can make choices that make you happy. Asking the question *Why?* all the time will not make you happy. What it will do is drive you to insanity.

There is no need to dig up the past. You do not need to analyze every little thing that happened to you in order to integrate and have a good life. Integration can happen in an instant. Traditional therapy wastes years taking us in the wrong direction in time.

EXERCISE

ASKING THE RIGHT QUESTION

Today observe yourself and pay attention to the moment you ask yourself or someone else the question *Why?* Then instead of asking yourself why, ask yourself a new question. Ask yourself, *What is it that I am doing in response to my experience?* Are you stuffing yourself with food? Are you looking for love in all the wrong places?

Once you become aware of the "what," then you can begin to change it. You can change the "what,"—the "why," you can't change. Ask yourself, *What can I do to be more empowered?* Or, *What can I do/think/ask, etc. that will be better for me?* And then act upon your insights.

LESSON
for Day Seven

WEEK ONE IN REVIEW

In Week One, you were introduced to and guided through five core concepts, all geared towards melting your resistance and getting the support of your mind, the part of you that is scared of change. This is important because you don't want your mind talking you out of the emotional changes that you are about to make.

The five core concepts were:

1. *Nobody Out There Will Come and Heal You.* You have the capacity to integrate your trauma and free yourself from its emotional imprint.

2. *Response-Ability.* You can learn to pause and reflect and to keep your heart open at all times.

3. *You Are Not Broken.* You might be confused about love, but there is nothing wrong with you. Your essence is love.

4. *What You Are Truly After Is Integration.* Trauma is not your enemy. As you integrate/digest it, it becomes the fuel for your growth.

5. *Stop Asking the Question Why?* You can't change the "why". Asking new questions, such as, What can I do to feel more empowered? brings you real change.

Next in the Blossom Journey, you will be gently guided to "land" within yourself by traveling out of the conceptual realm and into the sphere of your heart. Moving forward, you can listen as often as you wish to the guided "scientific" prayer and the downloaded meditation.

Exercise

Reflect Back

Reflect back at Week One of your Blossom Journey. Take out your journal and write your answers to these questions: *What was most helpful to you in this week's lessons? What kinds of shifts can you already see within yourself and in the beliefs you have been holding? What is starting to change in your life?*

Write what comes to you.

Week Two
LAND WITHIN YOURSELF

When most of my clients first come to me, they are used to living their life only from the neck up. That is, they *think* their way through life rather than *feel* it. When they have to make a decision, they listen to the advice that the voice in their head gives to them and not to the advice that their heart and intuition hold.

But they are not happy with the decisions they have made. They resist the life that they have created based on the calculations of their clever, protective minds. They are unhappy and driving themselves crazy with all their over-thinking, over-analyzing and trying to figure it all out.

When they come to me, they want me to tell them what they should do. The first thing I teach them is that I am not an oracle and I don't know what's good for them—no one outside of them ever will. Second, I tell them that they are fully capable of making good and healthy choices for themselves, and third, that the way they can feel safe again and make decisions that serve them is by being connected to their own intuition and following its voice. You can have contracts, weapons, or a lot of money, but when it comes down to it, only your intuition will keep you safe.

TAKING OFF FROM A NEW GROUND

You have begun your Blossom Journey by taking the first step of getting your mind on board and thus melting your resistance. In the last week, you took off from *old ground,* meaning the place where you feel most comfortable, the head.

You are prepared and ready now to land in new territory, a new ground within yourself, your feeling center. You are ready to redevelop your feeling capacity and learn how to process your emotions in a healthy way. This is the theme for this week and a necessary first step before you can access and trust your intuition. Both of these "new grounds" will bring you one step closer to opening your heart. Remember, the Blossom Journey is a journey from the mind to an open heart. You need to know how to appropriately "deal" with your emotions in order to be prepared for the theme and learning material for Week Three, Opening to Your Intuition.

Love, intimacy, and a feeling of safety can only come to you when you lead your life through your heart. Your heart is the bodily location from which your intuition speaks. Before you can hear and follow your heart, you need to learn how to filter out the other noise so you can hear and really listen to your heart.

LESSON
for Day One

BECOME THE OCEAN AGAIN

Before I continue, let me clarify what I mean when I use the phrase *feeling capacity*.

There are *feelings* and then there is a *feeling capacity*. They are two different things even though, in general, we think that they are the same. When we are having an emotion, or an emotion is having us, we think that we are feeling our feelings. Notice that I used the word *think* in the last sentence. The *thinking* is exactly what removes us from authentically experiencing the feeling. Feelings that are being thought about or reacted to are not being wholly felt. The only way to actually feel your feelings is to pause and be with them completely, to *sense* them physically and energetically in your body. This ability to authentically feel or sense your feelings is what I am referring to as feeling capacity.

Let's take a closer look at feelings and emotions before we dive into exploring the feeling capacity in depth.

What are feelings and emotions? From my experience, feelings are both physical and spiritual responses to what is happening either outside of us or within. Sometimes we have no control over them, and sometimes we don't feel anything. Many people have tried to get a grip on their feelings either through poetry, music or science. I have tried to suppress them or to express them in order to rule over them, both with very little success in terms of the degree of happiness I achieved.

Today I teach my clients that emotions and feelings are like the waves in the vast ocean and the only thing needed is to simply be with those that are yours and to let others have theirs. You will know when to act and when not. Feelings are energy, like food for the soul that feeds you but needs to be digested and transformed. The transformation happens through you digesting your emotional energy. The digestion happens through simply feeling the feelings using your feeling capacity.

The feeling capacity can be compared to an ocean. Think of that ocean as a big field within your soul, your being. It is the ocean that contains the waves, lets them go up and down, and let them be stormy or flat. The ocean doesn't judge, resist or deny the waves. The ocean doesn't get lost in each wave, either. The ocean is the space in which the waves occur. The ocean never loses itself—it stays the ocean whether the sea is stormy or flat. That ocean is like your feeling capacity, containing all emotions and feelings within yourself.

In a way, this week is all about learning to be an ocean again—mighty and free. Free to be a vast container for all that makes up *you*. Free to be a container for all of your experiences.

Unfortunately, you were taught to be a small pond. Let's look now at the reasons why you no longer are vast and free like the ocean.

How You Became a Small Pond

The first reason why you no longer are vast and free like the ocean is that you were taught not to be the ocean but to be a pond. We became ponds by denying, judging and resisting our feelings.

There are several things that contribute to you being a pond, not an ocean. One is that in today's society (and for a long time now), only positive feelings are welcomed. You have to constantly feel good and happy, or else it means something is wrong with you, and then people don't want to deal with you, and you get excluded. None of us wants to be alone and feel excluded, the need to belong being one of the strongest for all humans. We all got conditioned very early on about stuffing our emotions down.

When you stuff your emotions down, you unconsciously lie to yourself about how you are really feeling, and lying to yourself or someone else always leads to disconnection, and of course, *inauthenticity*. If you spend any time at playgrounds or around people with kids, you can observe how pervasive this "don't cry" attitude has become. I especially observed this attitude while spending time at various playgrounds when my daughter was very young. Little kids instinctively know what's good for their bodies and nervous systems if left to themselves. Whenever they are hurt, either physically or emotionally, their natural response is to cry. They cry, let it out of their system, and a little while later they are back in balance.

Many parents are uncomfortable with their children's crying, because they have learned to associate crying with unhappiness, that something is wrong. The truth is that children's crying is a physiological response to release stress from their system, from the body. Parents mean well when they comfort their child, no question. But what they actually do is send a message to the child that crying is not wanted, that "negative" feelings aren't welcomed.

Over time, children learn to control their emotions and lose the natural flow of energy between charge and discharge, and through that, a means of keeping the system healthy and in balance and staying in touch with themselves and others. Now the child's nervous system loses its means to discharge and self-regulate, and has to store the charge in its body. This takes up more and more energy and creates more disconnection. This happened and is still happening to most of us.

I am sure you have noticed how much energy little children seem to have available to them, and I am also sure that you have wondered why in the world you as a grown-up seem to have so little of it left in comparison.

One reason for this is that after living some years, we accumulate charge by not being able to express our true feelings. This charge needs to be stored somewhere. In other words, you use your body like a large garbage bin and put all your unresolved stuff in it, all the emotions that you had to stuff down. The bin gets fuller and fuller, and the amount of energy you need to keep the lid on, so it doesn't spill over, increases more and more. Keeping the lid on equals making sure this uncomfortable stuff stays out of your consciousness. This state of being is also called *denial*.

The energy that you once had available to you as a child to live, love, and enjoy life gets used to suppress the junk when you are an adult.

Now, when we as grown-ups see a child cry, the cries remind us of the full trashcan that we carry, and we don't like that a bit (again, this is all happening subconsciously). So we do everything in our power to make that sucker stop. We bribe, we shame, we scare—you name it. What we do to make a child stop crying is what people did to us when we were little to make us stop crying. Sadly, we don't just do it to others, but we have internalized the voices that told us to stop crying when we were little, and as adults we discipline ourselves. If we were simply left to ourselves, there would be no need to invent mechanisms to suppress our emotions. We wouldn't have had to find ways to get the garbage in the trash can and keep it there.

Another reason that you have less energy than a child is this: When you are first born, you are completely connected to everything and completely open, like a sponge soaking everything in. You feel like you belong to everything and everything belongs to you, you do not perceive yourself yet as separated from the world around you. Energies, feelings, colors, sounds—anything that your senses can perceive —moves through you, and it feels like you are it. Gradually you learn to distinguish what is *me* and what is *outside of me*. You learn from your parents or close caretakers what is accepted and what isn't.

You learned to listen to everyone but yourself.

Rather than taking clues from yourself and your intuition, you start disconnecting from yourself and taking clues from the outside world. When you do that, you automatically start closing your heart, because part of you is splitting off and denying itself. In psychological language, this process is called *dissociation*.

As a child, because your trashcan was fairly empty, you could simply put your emotions in it (suppress them). Most of us received training from our parents in how to do just that. Your parents most likely gave you pacifiers, sweets and punishments that helped you learn how to stuff your feelings. When you got older and the trashcan got fuller, you needed to come up with more than just throwing the trash in (suppressing the feelings and disassociating from yourself); no longer could you suck your thumb or hold your favorite stuffed toy. You then grabbed for more serious measures. Some of us started to drink, others became workaholics or super achievers, and others, like me, drowned their sorrow in food and serial boyfriends.

All of these things contribute even more to us disconnecting from ourselves and thus losing our power and energy. This is how we become the pond, how we become self-controlled, unhappy, beings capable of only small amounts of authentic feeling. It's a vicious cycle that gets passed on unconsciously from generation to generation. By waking up and becoming aware of it you can break this cycle.

As mentioned before, it's not only about waking up to the psychological damage but to the fact that by not crying and allowing all of your feelings to move freely through and out of you, you literally damage your physical body because you overload your nervous system. Your nervous system is the wiring that makes you function. The nervous system needs to release—it was not designed to store things like a trash can, a container that only gets charged and never discharged. And then things like smoking, over-eating, any of the mechanisms you may develop to suppress your feelings, are damaging your body further, in addition to the stress from non-release.

You having to constantly suppress your stuff, keeping the lid on the trashcan, is one of the main reasons you are contracted into a small pond. You are actually a vast, huge ocean contracted into a small focused pond that needs all its energy to stay compact, to not let anything out.

EXERCISE

KEEPING THE LID ON

Contemplate your answers to the questions and write them in your journal:

1. What do you do to not be the ocean, to contain yourself as a small pond? What are some of the mechanisms you use to stuff your emotions in the trashcan? (Do you smoke? Do you exercise excessively? Do you have lots of casual sex?)

2. Can you remember specific situations where you were upset, and you automatically did something to not feel upset, to "calm" yourself down? What happened and what did you do?

LESSON
for Day Two

YOUR FIRST LOVE IS THE DEEPEST

We are continuing with the theme of looking at the contributing factors that led to you becoming a small pond instead of staying a vast ocean. On Day One of this week of the Blossom Journey, we explored the societal contribution to how this happened, and today, we will look at a second cause. We are going to an even deeper level, beyond the conditioning you received after birth, to the conditioning you got before you were even born. We will look at what happened between you and your mother (your first intimate relationship) from your conception through birth.

The time you spend in your mother's womb and your birth shaped the way your nervous system developed and how you were wired for life, love, and intimacy. (Again, you will learn more about the nervous system and how trauma affects it in the next few weeks' lessons.)

In a healthy mother-child relationship, love flows uninterrupted between mother and child. In Family Constellation work, we call this open flow of life and love between mother and child the "uninterrupted reaching out movement." Picture a mother and her child, both entwined within open arms, their hearts united in love. It is the gesture a newborn makes towards its mother, towards life, and the gesture a "healthy" mother makes towards her newborn child.

Sadly, most of us don't have that. You probably didn't have that, and probably neither did your mom as a child. If you or she did, you wouldn't struggle so much with love, intimacy and your self-worth.

MOTHER EQUALS LIFE

For a newborn, mother equals life. Without mothers, there would be no life. People have an intact reaching out movement, if, when they were little, they learned that they could reach out, have needs, and get those needs met.

I know from my clients that most of them reached out over and over again, and weren't met with an open heart, weren't given what they needed, so they stopped reaching out. Most of my clients when they first come to me have to learn how to reach out and be open again.

You, too, probably experienced that interruption in what would have been a natural flow between child and mother, child and life, *you* and life. And you started to close down. It's a protection mechanism that we all have. The sad thing, though, is that by closing down, you slowly but surely lost your connection; first of all to yourself and what you need, and secondly to love and the people in your life. And then all the other things, like having to be a good girl, having to be strong, only showing happy feelings, etc., got layered on top.

One of my clients, Sarah, came to me because she just didn't seem to have any luck in love or in life. Sarah not only felt very lonely, but also struggled financially. From being involved with this work for so many years, I know that there is no such thing as a love or money problem. It always boils down to an inability to receive and be open. Sure enough, in the Family

Constellation that we did for Sarah, her mother came up, but Sarah could not accept that her mother was the one who gave her life. After we worked together for a while, Sarah was able to visualize her mother and say to her: *You gave me life.*

This sentence might seem like a trivial thing to say, since it is so absolutely, undeniably true. But for Sarah, being able to say this sentence was a quantum leap, and it influenced all her close relationships in a positive way.

In my work with groups, I have seen over and over again that the people who are able to restore their interrupted reaching out movement and heal the relationship with their mother are the ones who grow. They are able to reconnect with themselves and feel safe. In their power, they have a direct connection to their intuition, and stay open to allow true love and the right partner to come and stay.

The reconnection with my mother through my own reaching out movement was one of the biggest milestones I accomplished in my own healing process. When it was time for me to reach out, I couldn't. My arms were literally frozen, and I was stuck in the deep belief that she did not love me.

When I finally reached out in a therapy group and was able to say, *Mama, I need you*, when I finally allowed myself to feel that truth, it was as if a dam holding back a huge ocean had been released. So much sadness had been locked away in my heart.

I could feel how my adult need for food and confirmation through sex were so closely connected to this sadness. Being held by my mother was the sweetness and love I had *really* been longing for, not the substitutes I had been putting in its place.

It was interesting to realize that it was me who had stopped reaching out and not, like I had thought, my mom. She might have stopped sometimes, but I bet that there were many opportunities in my life where I could have reached out, whether it was to her or someone else, and received the soul nourishment I so needed. But I hadn't, I had resigned very early on.

I also learned that the experience wasn't so much about getting from my mother what, in my mind, I hadn't gotten. It was much more about my arms thawing and me realizing that at any point in life I can reach out—to anyone. Sometimes my needs will be met, sometimes they won't. But if I never reach out and never open up, it's guaranteed that I will never receive. This was a mighty lesson.

You Are the One Closing Down

Here is the kernel of this lesson for you: Whenever you don't feel loved by someone, most likely you are the one not loving and you are the one closing down your heart.

I remember the first week after the therapeutic connection with my mother, I felt so incredibly alive, connected, and in love with everything. I felt like I remember feeling when I was still a happy child. I could feel my essence of love, because all the roadblocks and all the negative beliefs about myself had been cleared away. The lid of my trash can was no longer holding back so much stuff and I was truly free.

Finding and cultivating this feeling of connectedness, of total aliveness and being in my power has become my life's commitment.

It's an illusion to think that you can get this by going back in time to become innocent again. It's not just an illusion, but in truth it is also not what you really want. You want to be like an innocent, happy, open-hearted child, but also to be conscious of that. As a child you are just who you are. Unaware. It is helpful to use the memory of who you were as a child as fuel for getting to a place of having an open heart again.

But in order to truly be free and who you are, you need to take it a step further and become both *childlike* and *grownup*. By childlike, I mean being able to be present in the moment with an open heart, just like a child. By grownup, I mean being able to respond to life rather than react, so that even when things hurt, you can stay conscious, process your emotions in a healthy way, and remember that you are love. That way, you act and live in a loving way that creates connection.

The more integrated you become, the greater becomes your capacity for being both more child like and grown-up.

EXERCISE

DISCOVERING YOUR SHUT DOWNS

Throughout the day, pay attention to the moments when you do not reach out but instead shut down emotionally. What are the circumstances? In the evening, take out your journal and write about your discoveries.

LESSON for Day Three

CORE WOUNDS

You are born into society's conditioning, you have your first experience of separation and interruption, and then you have especially traumatic experiences that seem to determine your entire life. In psychological language, these experiences are called core wounds.

I discovered my own core wounds only after I struggled in many relationships, always wondering why those relationships didn't work. As a little girl, I made a promise to myself that I would only marry out of true love. I would only marry my prince and no less. Not like all the grown up couples who had settled for less, who were so unhappy, who didn't talk with each other (or if they did, they only yelled and screamed).

Fast forward to my 26th year of life. Boyfriend X, who I am sure I'll marry and have a family with after only knowing him for three weeks, dumps me, and I am completely heartbroken. Again.

Then I meet this very nice man. He helps me get back on my feet. He cooks for me, spends time with me, is just nice, and things are easy. (You know what I mean: he calls, he's there, none of the usual drama.) We hang out and hang out, and hang out some more, and of course eventually one thing leads to another. We used birth control, but the universe had a different plan for us. After knowing him for only a couple of months,

I found out that I was expecting. We got married, we had our daughter, and we lived life together. We had our issues, but all in all we were a very good team.

If there just wasn't that promise that I had made to myself…

I just didn't feel anything. I didn't feel like I had been swept off my feet by my prince. I kept being pulled towards some other imaginary man. I would refer to him as "the love of my life," and I was convinced that he was still out there waiting for me. The one who would cherish me as if I were his most precious love, the one whose love for me was so steadfast that none of my moods or emotional storms would blow him away.

After our daughter turned four, and I finally had some time to be myself and not just be a mommy, I woke up one morning and realized that I had not been true to myself. I had not married out of love, and I had to rectify this. I took off my wedding band and presented my very surprised husband with my newfound truth. He had known that we had issues, but he never thought I would leave. He was shocked because he loved me very much. I separated from him and moved out and on with my life. (Or so I thought.) I wanted to have my own space, so that I could meet other men, and most importantly find my true love and have him stay with me.

I started dating, and every time the same thing would happen. It was actually the same thing that had been happening with men and me before I met my husband. I would fall in love, but the man did not. Every time I would think that he really was "the One," because, blah, blah, blah, blah, blah. And then he wasn't.

What I didn't know back then was this: You keep attracting the same people and situations over and over again, until you have healed your core wounds.

Eventually, my approach changed. I gave up on the whole "the love of your life is out there" thing and started buying into thinking that I had it "all" within me. I didn't need anyone out there to feel loved. I didn't need anyone to be happy. I tried being on my own, and being completely satisfied and happy with that for a while, but it didn't really make the longing for deeper love go away, either. I grew more desperate and afraid. I had read all the self-help books that promote the idea you must be fully happy on your own before you can attract true love. I doubted that I would ever get there.

Luckily, while I was going through this, my husband didn't stop loving me and wanting to be with me. Shortly after I had broken up with him, we found out that we were expecting again. To him, the fact that we were having another baby was a sign from God or a higher power that we belonged together. For me it was not. At that time, it simply annoyed me that he thought this was the case, and he just wouldn't go away. After a big fight in front of our midwife, I agreed to see a therapist, but just for the baby's sake. We went to see her, and her first question to me was, "Carolin, you told me that you are a therapist yourself, so when I ask you what your core wound is, you know what I mean, right?"

"Yes, of course I do," I said. "I was abused as a little girl."

Then the therapist says, "I hope you are aware that your problem is that you are still not trusting men…"

"Huhhh? I totally trust men. He's just not the right one!"

She pauses: "But he says he loves you, and he wants to be with you."

"No, he doesn't. He is just saying that. And either way, I don't care, because "the One" is still out there waiting for me."

After the session, I went home, very rattled within my paradigm. I started trying to translate what the therapist had said to me and came to the conclusion that even though I had spent half of my life in therapy and worked through just about every self-help book available, I still hadn't healed my past. Because of that, I wasn't able to see true love when it was right in front of my eyes.

My own core wound, and that of most of the clients who come to see me as a therapist today, was the result of my experience of childhood sexual abuse. In my case, that experience created the belief that people I love aren't safe, and being myself (radiant little female being) wasn't safe either.

After my first experience of core wounding, I encountered many situations in life where I trusted someone—my mom, my boyfriend, my best friend, a business partner—only to have that person stab me in the back, over and over again. It would happen with almost everyone who I "finally" trusted. It took me a while to figure out that those many events of betrayal and disappointment had all been the triggering of the same wounds, just in disguise. When it came to being married, I subconsciously had decided not to trust too much. I played it safe for many years by not letting my husband in too far. I was still in reaction to, and ruled by this, my core wound. But what I was actually longing for was a close connection with a man, my man, the man who was the father of my children.

I thought it was my husband's fault entirely, that he was too distant and not very emotional. I was very wrong.

In life, and I am sure you have experienced this over and over again, you seek out partners that match your core wound. They hold your pain right up in front of your nose, until you have integrated that pain and it can no longer rule you.

Core wounds are painful, but they do have a purpose. We all came here to earth wanting to learn something and wanting to grow towards our full potential, whatever that might be. Each of us came here with a very specific idea of what we wanted to experience in this lifetime, and what we wanted to check off as learned by the end of our life.

The way I see it, life basically writes the lesson plan. Our core wounds are the lessons.

Core wounds look a little different for each of us, but everyone has them. Mostly unaware, we choose our parents, and later on our intimate partners and our own children (if we have them), to help us heal our core wounds. These same people constantly remind us of those wounds by rubbing salt in them until they are all integrated, and we are made whole again.

Another name for core wounds is *emotional imprints*. As just explained, these imprints guide us to unconsciously pick the exact situations and people in life that we need in order to grow and evolve.

When I share this with my clients, it is a difficult concept to swallow at first, because it means on some level that they chose to meet the person who abused or molested them. On some level we, you and I, knew that we needed the traumatic experience or experiences we had in order to grow into the best we can be.

Through my own journey and by watching my clients blossom, I have learned that all that is necessary to integrate these imprints is to feel them. This is why it is so important to learn to be with your emotions. *Feel it to heal it.* Your feeling capacity is the skill you need to acquire in order to do that.

Feel it to heal it is a nice way to remember that in order for you to become free to be in the present moment, all it takes is to be with your emotions, to witness them, to cradle yourself, to give yourself empathy and to allow your emotions to simply flow through you. It's about learning to process your emotions and feelings in a healthy, natural way. There is no need to judge them, to justify them, or to mentally figure out why they are happening. It's not necessary to find out what their meaning is and what the stories attached to them are. There is no need to act them out or to react to them.

The only thing that is required of you is that you are present for them, like a loving mother is there when her child is having a tantrum. She would give her child the space to go through it. She sees her child having pain and sadness, and holds that child close to her heart, so she can cry the tears she needs to. No words or explanations are needed.

When the therapist told me I hadn't healed my own core wounds and that the dynamic between my husband and me was merely triggering that old hurt part of me, I was very doubtful at first. I just wanted to move on, and make my husband wrong and responsible for my aching heart. But another part of me wanted to heal, wanted to have the love of my life and wanted to live my vision of a happy family and life.

After being separated for more than eight months, on our 5th wedding anniversary, I decided to put my wedding band back on, and I made a commitment. The commitment wasn't to my husband, but rather to love itself. That was the moment I started walking along my own Blossom Journey. Just as the moment you committed to being love itself in the Prologue of this book was the beginning of yours.

The moment you are able to live as love and with an open heart, you will either realize that the love of your life has always been right in front of your nose, or it will show up and stay with you. I don't just mean this in an esoteric sense; I mean that the moment that you truly live with an open heart, your true partner will be there, to share it with you.

By committing to an open heart, you are also committing to a life in love. You're committing to honoring yourself and your emotions at the deepest level. In my opinion, this is the only life worth living.

Exercise

Committing to Love

Today you will continue to focus on becoming more and more aware of the energies that are going on within you. Pay attention again to the closing down, not reaching out, and the moments you open and your energies flow freely. As often as you can remember, and as it seems appropriate to the situation, repeat to yourself the following sentence: *I am learning how to process my emotions in a healthy way.*

In the evening take a few minutes and journal about your day.

Bonus

Did you commit to love before you started this journey?

If yes, journal about how that has been for you so far. If no, make that commitment now by returning to the Prologue.

Lesson for Day Four

RECONNECTING WITH YOUR WOUNDED INNER CHILD

Now that you know some of the reasons why your relationships and life might have been painful, why you keep yourself from feeling your feelings, and how important your connection to your hurt part is, let's continue to learn about how you can reconnect, integrate your wounds, and feel safe.

To land within yourself is the goal of this second week of the Blossom Journey, and it has everything to do with reconnecting with that part of you that was abandoned a long time ago.

This is the part of you that is most commonly referred to as your *wounded inner child.* You learned in Week One how this part wants to keep you safe and makes 80 percent of your decisions. It's part of your unconsciousness. The work of reconnecting with your wounded part in psychological language is called *inner child work.*

There are many very gifted therapists who focus on teaching inner child work. The main focus they all have in common is that in order for a person to successfully reconnect with their hurt inner child, they need to become their own loving parent. As long as you are looking to your birthparents to make things right, or as long as you blame them for all the things that went wrong in your life, you can't make this important step towards your own healing. It's mainly about being a loving parent to yourself and allowing whatever feeling you have to be valid without needing a mental justification. I know it may sound too simple to be true, but this ability alone will integrate, "heal" your emotional imprints and free up the energy that has been trapped in your emotional body, and thus in your physical body and life.

EXERCISE

INNER CHILD MEDITATION

Rather than giving you any more reading to do, I will take you on a guided mental journey. Make sure you have 20 minutes of uninterrupted time and space. Go to www.BlossomBook.com/ recordings and download the recording titled "Inner Child Meditation." Find a comfortable place, preferably lying down on your back. Have your journal and a pen nearby. You will be asked to take notes after you come out of the meditation.

LESSON for Day Five

MAKING PEACE WITH YOUR PARENTS

As I shared with you earlier, it is my belief that we all came to Earth because we made a conscious decision to develop ourselves further towards the full realization of love.

Part of that conscious choice was to choose the parents we have. Your parents are actually the people that make the biggest sacrifice and give the greatest gift that any human soul can give to you. Not because they spend many years and a lot of money and other resources on raising you and taking care of you, but because they are the ones most likely giving you the most pain.

Nobody likes creating pain for another human being, but your parents have no choice. They create your core wounds, because they are the ones you are first connected to and have to separate from to experience your self as an individual. If you are a parent yourself, you know how much you love your child. Nevertheless, you are the one causing the greatest wounds in your child by simply being the parent. Without core wounds, you or I or our children will never grow. Your parents give you the gift of growth. They give you the gift of life itself. It is up to you to do your work and turn what they have given you, the pain, into treasures. And of course, parents give you many, many wonderful things, too, and you as a parent give a lot of wonderful things to your children, I am sure.

The work is to integrate your earliest core wounds and to stop blaming your parents and your mother in particular for all that is bad in your life. It simply is a fact, a way of nature that parents "cause" core wounds. It is not their fault, there is nothing wrong with that or them, and they are neither evil nor mean. They are just people like you and me. It's how it's meant to be, and it's perfect that way. They give you the raw material so you can turn it into gold.

Without the lead, there will be no gold. Without their sacrifice of disconnecting from you, there would be no conscious intimacy and no paradise on Earth for you and me.

The work is also to release your parents from having to take care of you today, stepping up to the plate and starting to take good care of yourself.

Many of my clients who come to work with me feel that their parents owe them a better life, and some of them even wonder why their parents had them in the first place. Some even hate their parents, themselves, and their lives, because they are so convinced that since their parents weren't perfect, their lives are ruined.

I tell them that I have seen, over and over again through the Family Constellation work, that every human being does the best they can in any given situation. So do they, and so do their parents. Your parents' only job was to give you life, everything else is like whipped cream or icing on the cake. In order for you to be free and able to live a life in love, you must become your own loving parent and release your birthparents from their "obligation" of making life good for you. You are a grown woman, and you know how to make life good for yourself. You have the power to create the life you want.

You are now old enough to make life good for you.

Once I asked one of my spiritual teachers, "What is your daily practice?" He answered, "Being and staying present around my mother and my immediate family." Then he explained: "When you can enjoy the company of your birth family, you know you have made a good start towards freedom and the realization of love. Our mother is our greatest teacher. You don't need to worship me. Go home and live with your mother and worship her. Be thankful for any aspect not of love that she shows you by triggering your old wounds. It is the path to your freedom."

After I had gone through my own Blossom Journey, I actually moved back to Germany to be close to my mom and my family, to see if I had integrated my past. It turned out I had. The things that used to upset me didn't anymore, and my relationship with my mother is now open. I feel loved and supported, and I can completely let her in.

A wise person once said:

> "When we have father and mother in our hearts, we are rich people.
>
> When we have father and mother in our hearts, we are whole."

We then embrace all aspects of ourselves, masculine and feminine.

EXERCISE

RELEASING YOUR PARENTS

Today spend some time thinking about your parents and your life with them. Then write a thank you letter to each of them. If this is difficult, start with thanking them for your life. If even that is hard, write on a piece of paper why it is that you are not grateful for your life. Get all the blame out, and when you are done, rip or burn that paper. Then on a new piece of paper write down all the things for which you are grateful. Be with that list for a bit and realize that without your parents, none of this would be. Then go back to writing the letters to your parents. When you are done, you can choose to send it to them or to burn it—do whatever feels right.

LESSON
for Day Six

HEARING YOUR OWN NEEDS

Many of my clients find it relatively easy to reconnect to their inner wounded child, but they are more challenged by releasing their parents from having to take care of them and then learning to take care of their own needs. It's hard for us to become our own loving parent. Very few of us have had unconditionally loving, "perfect" ones.

You first have to realize that we are not perfect or unconditional, either, but that we can strive for it. You can become your own loving parent by listening to your own needs. Here is the problem for most of us: Especially as women, we don't know what our needs are anymore. We have learned to put everyone else first. Many of my clients spend weeks on this step, the rediscovery of their own needs.

The tool that I teach my clients and that they find very helpful in regard to being able to hear their own needs again is called the Non-Violent Communication (NVC) process. It was first developed by Marshall Rosenberg to help people in their conflicts with others. I myself find it most helpful as a tool to check in with myself in my own inner conflicts.

I'm not going to attempt to teach you this process of communication in depth, but I encourage you to go to the official website (www.CNVC.org) and do some research. If you want to learn it, I am sure you can find a study group or class in your area. The NVC community is growing rapidly. I will give you a brief overview of the basic NVC process in this lesson, enough so that you can start using it for the same purpose I have used it, to be able to hear your own needs.

At the base of NVC is the premise that we all have needs that are equally valid. If we can understand a person's true needs, we create connection. We generally don't communicate in a way that is clear about these needs. We usually don't communicate in a non-accusative, non-violent way in order to get what we want. What we usually do is take our "want" and turn it into an order or a hurtful message to make the other give us what we demand.

Let me give you an example. Let's say you feel tired and your lover walks in the room and wants something from you. I think it's safe to say that your response would be something like, "Leave me alone!" But you probably meant this: "I am feeling tired, and I need space."

But given your more contentious outburst, would your partner have gotten the message about what you really needed? Would he have been able to understand that you were tired and that you needed space, or would he just have been pissed off at your grumpy mood? Most likely the latter is the case.

Marshall Rosenberg calls our normal way of communicating Jackal language. A jackal is a wild animal resembling a dog, but in this case the term refers to a tough guy who can't express his needs and feelings simply the way they are; he has to package them into a message that makes the other person wrong. It is very rare that a person doesn't feel attacked by our need when it is communicated in this disguised "jackal" way.

It takes practice to hear the needs of another beyond the message that is so easily perceived as attacking you.

The non-violent communication process is a simple four-step process. The steps are:

Observation

Feeling

Need

Request

Let's look at how you can use these as steps to listen to and hear your needs.

First, adopt an approach of listening emphatically to yourself by stating an observation, which is the most neutral thing you can say about any issue. (I will clarify this point in a minute.) Then, make a guess about the feelings and needs you may have. After that, make a request to yourself.

Here is an example: My client Ruth called me on the phone, completely beside herself having just backed into a wall at a beach parking lot. She was calling herself crazy, a lunatic, all kinds of things. I asked her to pause for a minute and tell me the neutral observation (step #1) of what had just happened. She then said, "Instead of stepping on the brake, I stepped on the gas pedal, and the car made a jump and landed at the wall."

Then I said, "I am guessing you are in shock (step #2, guessing her feelings)." She said, "Yes, I think you are right. It was pretty scary." Then I said, "I am guessing you need someone to help you (#3, guessing her underlying need)?" She replied, "I just need some time to be with myself (#4, a clear request she could make of herself)." Ruth then went to the beach where she sat quietly for a while, getting her need for quality alone time met, and then took care of her car later.

In this example, I helped Ruth connect to her true need by using *observation, feeling* and *need,* and facilitated her to come up with a request to herself of going to sit alone on the beach and gather herself before dealing with the problem.

This process helps you to uncover your own true needs, and because of that, you build trust with yourself. More than anything, non-violent communication helped me to connect with my inner child, my needs, my intuition, and my heart. To me it is the most valuable inner child work tool, and I encourage you to explore it further in the resources available either online or in your community.

A WORD ON CATHARSIS

Throughout my training as a Humanistic Psychotherapist, I have participated in several inner child workshops that focused on helping me to access my anger and let it out by screaming, yelling and even strangling my parents—dolls or pillows representing them. Though it felt good in the moment to be allowed to express all that energy, it left me empty and somewhat feeling like I had just been run over by a truck. Because of my own experience with these modalities, I started doubting that they were effective.

Here is what I have come to believe. Catharsis is still advocated in many forms of modern psychotherapy. It has its place if you want to experience yourself completely out of control. If you want to experience all of who you are, the wild, the screaming, the raging part, etc. But if your main goal is to integrate your stuff and to heal, other measures are required. We will talk later about why that is, when we take a close look at trauma and the nervous system.

EXERCISE

HEARING YOUR OWN NEEDS

Today and moving forward, practice hearing your own needs by using the NVC process. Write your dialogues down in your journal, following the four steps, whenever you are upset or conflicted about something. You will discover that your upset is often due to an unmet and unacknowledged need, and underneath that, a simple request will give you what you truly want.

LESSON for Day Seven

WEEK TWO IN REVIEW

In this second week of your Blossom Journey, you continued to move out of your head and into your heart. You learned that in order to get to your authentic and powerful state of being, you must integrate your emotional imprints, those core wounds that were created early on through your relationship with your parents and with your abuser. You also learned that integration can only occur when you learn to use your feeling capacity again, and when you learn to process your emotions in a healthy, natural way.

You learned that:

You became a little pond because of the conditioning you received. You keep yourself small with mechanisms that help you to stuff your emotions down.

Your first love, the one for your parents, is the deepest. All your intimate relationships reflect back what still needs to be healed in this first intimacy.

Only when you integrate your core wounds can you be free. You do this by simply allowing yourself to have your feelings— not stuffing them.

Parents give you the gift of life. Everything else is whipped cream on the top. When you have your parents in your heart, you are rich.

You must become your own loving parents. The way you do that is by learning to listen to your needs, and by fulfilling them.

Now that you have started to reconnect to your inner child and bring peace to your heart, you are ready to reestablish a safe and trust-filled connection with yourself through the voice of your intuition. Learning how you can hear your intuition, and be sure that what you are hearing is truly it, will be the next step on your Blossom Journey. Later on in the journey, your intuition will help you know when it is time to just sit and integrate an old imprint. The situations you need to integrate are the situations where you normally react, and act out, what you think are your feelings. Steps 1 through 4 of the Blossom Journey are geared towards preparing you for learning the integration procedure, which will be presented in depth in Week Five.

EXERCISE

REFLECT BACK

Reflect back on Week Two of your Blossom Journey. Take out your journal and write your answers to these questions: *What was most helpful to you in this week's lessons? What kinds of shifts can you already see within yourself and in the beliefs you have been holding? What is starting to change in your life?*

Write what comes to you.

Week Three
OPEN TO YOUR INTUITION

In the last week, you learned about, and started to re-access, your feeling capacity. You also started to reconnect to your inner child, because ultimately it is the wounded part of yourself that needs to be seen and integrated so you can become whole. It was your inner child that wasn't allowed to feel what you were feeling. But this part of you is fully capable of feeling and still knows exactly how it is done, once permission is granted.

Week Three of your Blossom Journey is all about using your feeling capacity to connect to your intuition, the voice of your heart. You will learn that only when you have access to that voice can you be guided by your Higher Self, the eternal part of yourself, and be completely safe.

Your intuition is always your trusted advisor. This week you will first look at all the different parts of your make up, so that you can recognize the voices that empower you and the ones that disempower you, and differentiate between them. Second, you will learn energetic tools that help you to know beyond the shadow of a doubt how it feels when you are connected to your intuition. This will enable you to make wise and healthy choices in life, and to end the drama. Lastly, you are strengthening your new muscle, your feeling capacity, because you are using it to access your intuition, and, as you know, the more we use a muscle, the stronger it gets.

LESSON
for Day One

YOUR HIGHER SELF

Today let's look at how "the heart always knows" as a first step towards learning to hear your intuition and access your Higher Self.

The reason why the heart always knows is because it is in direct connection to your Higher Self. Your Higher Self is that part of you that simply always is. It is that part of you that can never be destroyed, that part of you that is always love and freedom. The Higher Self is the part that you slowly forgot when you incarnated into your body, and the qualities of which you seek to realize during your life on earth.

Your Higher Self doesn't have an ego. Because it has no ego, it also doesn't fear death. It is free of fear, just as your pure heart. Your Higher Self knows how to put the experiences you go through into perspective. It may even be the one arranging the experiences so that we as earth beings can evolve and grow. Your Higher Self is not constrained by time or space or human condition, therefore it always knows.

As I did with you, I always tell clients not to believe blindly in what I say, but to test it. When they have a conflict with their child or their mother or partner, and they feel like they have been talking to a wall for quite some time, I teach them about their Higher Self, and I send them home to try out what you are about to practice today. Every time they do, they come back and tell me how astonished they are that it worked.

You, too, can experiment with this practice. It works because your Higher Self is wisdom itself. You can absolutely rely on it, your own advice, when you have learned to listen to the "right" voice.

Your Higher Self speaks to you through the voice of your heart, your intuition. It speaks to you through symbols, other people and circumstances, dreams, and many other vehicles. Your heart is the organ that deciphers your Higher Self's coded messages.

There was a time in my life when I had a difficult time listening to my own heart whenever a guy was involved. I would so desperately want him to be "the One", to marry him and have kids together. I thought it was all about the guy, but in the end it was really about surrendering to love and trusting my own intuition.

Life has a funny way of guiding us towards the fulfillment of greater love. At the time, I was still living in Germany. One night I came home to my apartment that I was sharing with a friend to find out she had an old acquaintance visiting, a former high school exchange student from the U.S. who was staying for the night. We all hung out, had a great time, and I ended up spending the night with him (that's what we sexually abused women do, we jump into bed too quickly). The next day he left to go back home to America. I was in love, of course, because we'd had sex. I was in love with an American. I never would have thought that America and I would become close.

When faced with the decision to follow him, to leave everything behind, go to America and follow my heart, I was conflicted. I had worked so hard to gain my independence financially and emotionally. I wasn't sure whether the voice of my wounded inner two-year-old was talking to me or my heart. As long as I was focusing on him, whether he was "the One" or not, I couldn't make a decision.

At that time I was working with *A Course in Miracles*, a book and self-study curriculum that contains spiritual wisdom and was channeled and written by Helen Schucman and William Thetford in 1976. I decided to let the book speak to me and in doing so, help me to decide. As I mentioned earlier, your Higher Self can communicate to you in many ways if you are open and if you know how to recognize it. At the time, I was studying how to get in touch with my Higher Self, so I opened the book and read: "God is love, and therefore so I am, I will step back and let him guide the way."

Upon reading these words, I got a clear sense of a *yes* feeling in my belly, a yes to the truth that the book's pages had opened. All of a sudden my decision wasn't about the guy anymore. It was about love. It was about following my heart. And my heart was telling me to go. Did I marry that the guy? No, I didn't. Was it the right thing to come to America? Absolutely—yes!

EXERCISE

HIGHER SELF MEDITATION

The person who introduced me to the concept of working with the Higher Self was author and transformational leader Shakti Gawain. In her book, *Creative Visualization,* she offers a beautiful meditation to connect with the Higher Self. I have recorded my own version of that meditation for you. Go to www.BlossomBook.com/Recordings for the download. The meditation takes about 20 minutes to complete. Have your journal nearby, and after meditating, jot down notes about anything that comes to you.

BONUS

Do this additional exercise if you are dealing with a conflict with another person. Close your eyes and picture your Higher Self talking to theirs. Communicate. Listen to what their Higher Self has to say, and share your own truth with theirs. The next time you meet with that person in real life, observe any changes in them, yourself, or your relationship with them.

Lesson for Day Two

Your Subconscious Make Up

When you are born, you are a pure bundle of light, of love and complete innocence. You have nothing but your parents or in their absence, the ones who stepped in to take care of you. You are like a sponge—open and soaking up everything that comes to you. If you are lucky, you get dealt a good hand of cards: loving, conscious parents, a stable environment, and lots of protection. If you aren't so lucky, you have to learn on your own to protect yourself.

Actually, just being born—coming out of the womb where you were fully protected and taken care of and no longer living in a world of unconditional love—requires that you protect yourself so your heart won't break and the pain totally kill you. To do that, you started creating other parts of yourself. You moved out of wholeness into separation, into fragmentation. The other parts perceived themselves as all that you are. Their main function became to keep you safe.

In this second lesson of Step 3, you will learn about the many parts of your subconscious and get familiar with their different voices. You will not only learn about them, but get to know them so well that you can make proper use of some and fully embrace others. Again, the goal of Step 3 of the Blossom Journey is to learn how you can know when you are talking to your trusted advisor, your heart, and when not—when you are listening to your head and the voices of all those different parts.

I teach my clients that each of us has these parts. And that each of these parts has a function within our psyche. Some of the more well known ones are the *inner child, wounded child, inner critic,* the voice of your mother, and the voice of your father. You'll get to work with some of these voices in this book; others you are invited to explore on your own. All of these parts live in your subconscious and it is the sum total of these that make you *you.*

As I mentioned, many of these voices live in your subconscious mind. The dream place. The shadow. That place that stays hidden from sight in your ordinary life. It is the ninety-percent of the iceberg that you can't see, hidden under water.

YOUR SAFETY PATROL: EGO

The predominant structure in your psychological make up is your *ego.* The ego enables you to function in the world, with its main goal being to keep you safe. It's most often the "I" that you define yourself as. (E.g. I am five foot, six inches tall, and I have blonde hair.)

The ego is the "I" that lives in your mind and talks to you through all the many voices. It guides you through life via adapted and acquired beliefs. Many of those beliefs and remembered experiences are very useful, such as *fire is hot and you'd better not touch it.* Others hinder you in the fulfillment of your true desire, such as *love always hurts, so you'd better stay away from it.*

The ego also acts like a giant filter determining what you will become aware of and what you will not, all based on past experiences and on emotional imprints that haven't yet been integrated. If you have a belief that you are not good with love because you once lost someone you loved deeply, your ego will do everything to keep you from even trying to have anything to do with love again. It's the same with money, health and other areas. Unless you become aware that your belief is based on the fact that you once got hurt, and that it is not true that you are bad with love, money, etc., you will continue living your life in a limited way.

Your ego is more or less composed from experiences you had, decisions you made, and beliefs you adopted from the time when you were less than three years old. It is this early structure that is mostly running your life, that believes and tries to make you believe that what was true for a two-year-old girl is still true for a 20, 30, 40, 50, 60 something-year-old woman.

Does the ego need to die? In many spiritual traditions, the "death of the ego" is seen as a goal to aspire to. It is seen that true love lies beyond the ego and so the ego must go.

The truth that I have come to is that we as human beings couldn't live without our ego. If our ego were to die, we would be overwhelmed by the world. We do need time and space to be able to orient us, to keep from going crazy. Time and space are constructs of the ego. What serves us most is to let the ego help us find our way around but not let it make crucial decisions for us.

EXERCISE

THANKING YOUR EGO

During your day, pay attention to how your ego is serving you and start acknowledging and thanking your ego for that. Write your observations in your journal.

LESSON
for Day Three

END THE DRAMA

For most of the people who come to me, life seems to be very exhausting and unfair. They tell me that it feels like everything is up to them. It's up to them to keep their marriage together, it's up to them to create peaceful family time, and it's up to them to even have successful date nights. Nothing seems to just flow easily and harmoniously. There is always drama. And their partner, husband or lover holds them responsible for it. I often hear about women whose husbands call them a drama queen. And, of course, they feel hurt by that.

Here is the thing: In most cases, the husbands are right about the drama queen thing. In my case, when I was called that, I got very angry, because I didn't like to be told that I was a drama queen. I didn't know, though, that because of my past history, I was wired for it. Today I know that when trauma happens, our nervous system gets wired for drama. I will share with you how exactly that happens later in this week. What I have also learned is that when people call you a drama queen, they most likely want you to stop acting unloving to yourself and to them.

A helpful way of looking at drama is through the lens of our energetic bodies. The well-known author and spiritual teacher Eckhart Tolle explains in his book *The Power of Now* that drama is like this: We all have a *pain body*. This pain body is almost like an entity unto itself. It feeds off negative energy. We are its host. Whenever our pain body gets hungry, it needs us to get involved in some kind of emotional drama, so it can feed off the negative energy that the drama creates.

The pain body is the emotional body with all its emotional imprints—the trash can full of garbage with the lid tightly shut. The more you integrate your emotions, the less energy your pain body has, because it is literally starved to death when left with nothing on which to feed. The less energy your pain body has, the less drama you create.

When the pain body is active, it takes you over and makes you feel like you are *it*. It uses your ego to talk to you. Because of this, it has total control over you via your emotions (the feelings of a scared two- or three-year-old child). When you are in the grip of your pain body, drama feels good, because all the energy makes you (aka your pain body) feel alive.

You know you have fallen prey to your pain body's feast when you can't stop fighting and being right, and when you are completely exhausted by your drama afterwards.

We, as women, are especially challenged in this way around our monthly period. Pain bodies are very active around that time, and I am sure you can attest to that one! There are two reasons for this, and the first one is that the collective pain body of women is more loaded because of all the injustice that has happened to us throughout history. The second one is that we as women are the more emotional gender. Ironically, because we have a stronger experience of the pain body through being more emotional than men, we as women have an easier time when it comes to being love, being conscious of our emotions, and integrating them. The explanation for this is that in order to integrate, you need to *feel,* and as women, we have easier access to our emotions. Again, integration is the key to stopping drama and trauma.

One word of caution: a life void of drama might at first feel empty and boring, but this is only your pain body speaking — it is going through withdrawal and wants to get you to engage in drama again, so it can get fed. It is important to be aware of this.

Trust me, it is much more satisfying to feel alive through real encounters of intimacy and love than through reactive emotional drama. The voice of your *inner wise woman* can be like a buoy in stormy seas, helping you out of the storm of overflowing emotions and back to calm and healthy ground. It's an energetic feeling that I encourage you to start paying attention to.

YOUR INNER WISE WOMAN

The counterpart to the ego and the pain body, if you will, is your innate intelligence, which I call your *inner wise woman*. This part of you knows how to be present and in truth, knowing that we are all here to be love and to live in love.

Your inner wise woman does not need drama. It sometimes even feels emotionally flat when you first connect to her. Your Higher Self pushes you towards the realization and use of this part the older you get by putting you into situations that trigger your core wounds. The situations might have different players and different circumstances, but in the end it is all the same old hurt. Until you integrate it.

Your inner wise woman is the part of you that can let you know when you are triggered and help you to integrate your core wounds. When you are in the midst of a painful reaction and you do not understand that the pain is the triggering of old wounds, you are like a puppet—un-free and run by the past.

You remain this way as long as you don't know you have an inner wise woman who you can trust to guide you through the integration work.

I teach my clients that the most important thing they will ever do in their life is to gain the ability to see the hurt for what it is and to transform it into freedom and love. Integration and getting to a place where it is safe for you to have an open heart is, ultimately, really simple. I like to use the words of my beloved husband here, who often says, "The way out is the way in." But so few people know this, or if they do know it, they don't dare go there. If you dare, your inner wise woman awaits.

EXERCISE

PAY ATTENTION TO YOUR INNER VOICES

Identify some of the voices that you listen to, specifically your pain body, your wounded little one. Listen for your inner wise woman as well. Throughout your week, pay attention to your voices and journal about them. See if you can identify your pain body as a separate creature that lives off your emotionally negative energy. See if you can sense when you are either searching for love from the place of the scared little child or making decisions from your grounded wise woman's place.

In addition, get curious and sharpen your observation in an attempt to get glimpses of other parts that are active within your soul. Parts with voices that give you advice to which you listen. Where do they come from? Are they useful to you or hindering your truest desires? Write any of your insights from this in your journal.

LESSON for Day Four

MOVING FROM FRAGMENTATION INTO WHOLENESS

For you to be able to hear your intuition, it is important to move out of your fragmentation into your wholeness. Yesterday, you learned to hear the voices your fragmented parts use and also learned about their antidote. Today you will get clear on your purpose as a last step before connecting to your intuition.

FINDING MY PURPOSE

A story about my own experience of finding my purpose illustrates today's lesson. When I was around 22, I remember having an identity crisis that had to do with my purpose in life. I had been focusing on my relationship with my boyfriend at the time for many, many years, and it seemed that the more I tried to make it work, the less it actually did. I was far from feeling fulfilled, so instead of focusing on my relationships, I started focusing on other areas of my life. I wanted to find myself.

I left high school at the age of 16 and had made money in different ways, including starting my own businesses and waiting tables at night. My first business was a decorative painting business, my second a catering service. I tried to define myself through these businesses, but it hadn't been working. Then one night—I was 21— I was waiting tables as usual, and a friend of my boyfriend came into the restaurant. Business was slow. He recognized me and since he didn't have any other plans for that night, he decided to keep me company, so I wouldn't fall asleep on my feet.

Soon, it was midnight. I don't know what came over me, but I told this stranger my entire life story. I told him how I'd had my "toilet wake up" moment and basically healed myself from my eating disorders with the help of the Family Constellations work I'd done.

After he listened for well over an hour, he simply said, "Well, if you have been able to heal yourself, then you must make your life about teaching other women and girls how they can heal themselves, too." With that he left, and I never saw him again. But what he had said left a deep impression on me. Shortly after that night, I decided to become a Naturopathic Doctor and Humanistic Psychotherapist.

I thought I had finally figured out who I was and what my purpose was. But something within was still restless, always wanting to know which "one thing" I *really* was. I wanted to be able to pinpoint whom I was in one simple sentence, like others can, saying, "I am a doctor" or "I am a school teacher." To simply say, "I am Carolin," just never seemed enough.

Back then, I felt that if I could accomplish being the one defined thing, I would finally have returned to a normal state of being. I would feel whole, know my purpose, gain my parent's approval, and fit in with society. My loneliness would be over and I would be loved.

My search continued. After I left my long-term codependent relationship, I decided it was time to live my dreams and go traveling. As mentioned before, I never felt at home in Germany and was always looking to find my true home. I had some idea that it was a warmer country where people were more guided by their hearts, like the more southern Europeans.

I kept hearing about a special island—*La Gomera, La Gomera.* In my research I found out that La Gomera was the second smallest of the Canary Islands off the west coast of Africa in the Atlantic Ocean. Rumor had it that Atlantis used to be there in olden times before it sunk beneath the waves.

I fell in love with the idea of La Gomera, booked my flight, and packed all my belongings. And when I say *all* my belongings I mean ALL. And I went.

La Gomera, I'd learned, was a total backpacker's paradise. I had a vision of me going into nature and finding God or whatever I was looking for, and of course also "the One" while I was there. I would have one week to explore the island and its magic, before the second week when I'd booked a Family Constellation retreat at a local retreat center. I felt I'd needed to bring my entire wardrobe just in case I met "him." I needed to have choices to make myself especially attractive.

My idea was to get there, with a suitcase, my backpack and my camping equipment, and go climbing into the mountains by myself. Then, I'd sit there all by myself and finally find enlightenment, the truth about me, and my life and love.

Okay. But here is how it really went down. It still makes me smile about myself and about what we women do in search of love. What was I thinking???!!!

First I had to fly to Tenerife, one of the bigger Canary Islands, which is a five hour flight from Germany. When I got there, I had to wait half a day to ride a bus half way across the island, then take a four hour ferry across the Atlantic Ocean and then another three hour bus trip from one side of La Gomera to the other.

By the time I arrived in Valle Gran Ray (the Valley of the Great King), my chosen destination, I was extremely exhausted from lugging all my belongings. When I got off the bus, it dawned on me that I had no clue, no map, none of the right gear, didn't know anyone, and was completely overloaded with clothes. It was getting dark quickly.

Valle Gran Rey was the last bus stop, and during the ride, I'd noticed another woman traveling on her own, but unlike me, she seemed to be familiar with the people and land. She was the only one who stayed on the bus with me until the end. I mustered all my courage and asked her what she would do in my situation. It turned out that she was one of the people living and working at the retreat I'd be attending. She suggested that I go there and find out if I could check in a week early. I somehow found enough strength to walk the one mile dirt road leading from the bus stop through the steep, mountainous coastline to the retreat center.

The retreat center was tucked in the last corner of civilization. I was able to book a tent stay. Needless to say, I was extremely happy. I very quickly forgot about my lonesome vision quest in the mountains. My love for fashion had outweighed my search for enlightenment. Well, that's not entirely true. I did spend a lot of time alone and in silence, and got some good answers to my questions. It also turned out that it was good I'd brought all my clothes, because in the end they helped me to attract a very sweet man. He noticed me partly because I was not dressed in the uniform of yoga pants or hemp like everyone else. He was a musician and the maintenance guy for the retreat center. We fell in love on my last day.

I was still in search of my wholeness and purpose. A few months later, I returned and ended up living with him and being part of the retreat center staff. We lived in a small hut on the far end of the retreat center garden, a piece of land that was wedged between the wild Atlantic Ocean and the steep wall of red mountains. Everything there was amplified. Everything was very raw and primal.

There was a reason for this retreat center being so special and different. It came out of a commune that had been founded by disciples of Osho, also known as Rajneesh, one of the great spiritual teachers from India of the late 20th century. My personal relation to him is through my mother who became a disciple and traveled to India shortly before my parents' marriage broke apart. Osho's disciples are also called the "orange people," because of their orange clothing. Osho was a teacher of ultimate freedom which resulted in many of his students living in non-attachment to anyone and practicing free sex. The man I was with had been Osho's musician for a while when he was in his twenties. When I met him he was in his 50s and had returned to a monogamous life. Nevertheless, some of the people in the commune hadn't. Many walked around half-naked during the day and practiced all kinds of forms of free expression.

While I was living at the "finca," the retreat center, a spiritual teacher from Holland visited, and I had the opportunity to ask her a question during *satsang*, which is the ceremony where you sit quietly with a master and get to ask your most burning questions. "I've been studying and working toward my degrees in naturopathic medicine and humanistic psychotherapy for over three years now," I said, "but I am not sure if I am a Naturopathic Doctor or a therapist, and whether I want to be that for the rest of my life. I don't know who I am and what my purpose is—please help me!"

The wise woman's reply was so deep it shook me to the core. She explained to me that one of the silliest things our society does is to expect young ones to know in their 20s who they want to be for the rest of their life. She said: "The truth is nobody knows who they will be, tomorrow, next year, or in ten years. Everyone is many things in one life. As a matter of fact, you are many things at any given moment in time. You are many things at once, and over time and at the same time, you are one constant. The constant is that you are an expression of love and your purpose is the expression of love. When you live your purpose of love, it doesn't matter which form it takes, whether you are a bus driver, a cook, a teacher, or just yourself."

This really was a new concept for me. I realized that I had been searching for the wrong thing—I had been searching for the *form*, rather than the *content* of my purpose in life. This knowledge provided great relief for me. It allowed me to see myself in a much bigger context and also made me realize that in order for me to be truly who I am and experience true love from a place of my power, I don't need to be one thing but rather live from all my different sides, explore them and love them all. I need to integrate all the fragments so I can be whole.

I ultimately left my sweet lover and the finca after nine months, because I had bigger plans than living on a small island far away from civilization and freely expressing myself.

I would have loved to take my lover with me, but it just wasn't meant to be. But he taught me what it feels like to be in a truly loving relationship, one without drama where love just flows. For that, he has a very special place in my heart.

But back to you and your journey. I wanted to share this story in its fullness, because it illustrates a very important point, which is that our restless search for purpose is really our fragmentation made visible. By fragmentation, I mean the state of having traveled out of your body and into your mind with its many separate voices.

EXERCISE

FINDING YOUR PURPOSE

Play with the concept of your purpose being love. See how you can express this purpose in your work, at home with your friends or even when you buy groceries. In the evening, reflect on how it felt to you and what shifts within yourself and your interactions with the world you were able to notice. Write your insights in your journal.

LESSON for Day Five

CONNECTING TO YOUR INTUITION

Now that we have explored some of the reasons why your heart always knows, have looked at some of the voices and energies you have within, and gained some perspective on what contributes to your fragmentation, let's take a closer look at intuition and how we can use our feeling capacity to get a clear connection to it.

This day's lesson is about your intuition. Some people think they don't have any, but the fact is, everyone has this internal guidance system. The seat of intuition is in the heart. It might not talk as loudly or convincingly as the mind, but when you learn to listen to your intuition, your life will seem to flow and be touched by grace.

We are not used to listening to our intuition. The ego is more predominant and wants to keep you safe. The voices of your mother and father for example, which are instilled deeply in you, are the ones you are used to listening to, simply because they were the ones guiding you while growing up and you have heard them the most. Unfortunately, no one teaches you when you are young that the source of your wisdom lies within, that you indeed are the only one who knows what is good for you.

As discussed earlier, you are trained to take your cues about whether what you are or, what you do, is right or wrong from sources outside yourself. Speaking from experience, life can be very magical and wonderful when lived from intuition. I often marvel at the way things unfold. But this only happens when I trust and follow my heart.

It takes a firm commitment to take yourself seriously, and to honor yourself.

We always have a choice to look at things either from a mental perspective or from a heart perspective. Often you aren't sure from which perspective you are looking, because you are so tangled up in your emotions. To make a decision in a difficult situation or to make any decision with the support of your trusted advisor, your intuition, you have to use your body and your feeling capacity.

Your body gives you very clear feedback. It does this through your true *yes* and *no*.

Your true yes and no is what your integrated self wants. Your inauthentic, non-true yes and no is your automatic response, when you say yes but mean no, and no when you mean yes. Your body gives you very clear feedback about your true yes and your true no; you just have to relearn to read it and to accept it.

FEELING YOUR TRUE YES AND NO

How do you feel your true yes and no? For most of us this is hard to do because we are so used to making decisions either based on a "pro and con" list or on logic. But the truth often doesn't have anything to do with logic. Your true yes and no is a sensation in your body. Since it is a sensation, it tends to be rather quiet. Your mind can easily out-scream it. This is why you need your feeling capacity in order to listen to it.

You probably know of situations where you haven't listened to your body's cues and have gotten ill and so you have some idea of what I'm talking about. The way your body conveys an authentic yes or no may be subtle, but if ignored will develop over time into more severe physical symptoms. Until you can no longer stop paying attention or else you might die.

The idea is to learn to hear your body's messages early on so you don't have to develop physical symptoms. Then, you can be healthy, vital and at peace.

To give you an example: When guided through the exercise below, one of my clients reported back that her *no* felt like a knot in her lungs, and her *yes* felt like an opening in the chest. Over time, she learned not to make a decision unless she had a clear sense of either.

I invite you to find that place in you, in your body, where you feel, without a doubt, whether you are on the right track or not. This step is very important. Almost all the women I have worked with nod in agreement when I ask them if they tend to say yes quicker than they can think. For many of my clients, learning this piece completely shifted their life.

Listening to your true yes and no requires that you pause before you open your mouth. If you respond to a request within seconds, you can be sure you didn't take the time to check in with yourself. Take your time and let people know that you need a moment or a night before getting back to them. Make this a new habit.

The more you practice paying attention to your true yes and no, the easier listening to your intuition becomes. The side effect of a stronger growing connection with your intuition is that you start feeling safer. When you feel safe, you can relax into your being - into love, into wholeness - Then your life feels touched by grace and the drama begins to vanish.

My invitation to you today is to not only pay attention to the little and the big moments when you say yes and mean no or you say no and you mean yes, but to take it one step further and act upon your bodily feeling of your true yes and no. Checking in with your body before you commit is a learnable skill. As with any other skill, it takes practice. The more you are able to be in touch with yourself and express what you really feel and want, the more you'll be able to trust yourself. Then your inner child can trust your grown up self, relax and let the guard down. When that happens, you can experience closeness and intimacy, because the voices in your head aren't telling you to play it safe anymore. They know they are safe with you. They know you make healthy and good choices now. As a child, it was different, as you weren't capable of deciding. You often had no choice. Now you have one.

In any moment you have the choice to ask yourself, *Is this right for me or not?*

You have the choice to allow the answer and to act on it. You are the only one who can.

EXERCISE

DISCOVERING YOUR TRUE YES AND NO

Today's exercise comes in two parts. Part one is learning what your true yes and no feel like. To help you with that, I have recorded a guided meditation to get you in touch with your true yes and no. This meditation takes about 10 minutes. Go to www.BlossomBook.com/recordings, download and listen to the recording.

Part Two: Throughout your day pay attention to how quickly you respond. A great place to test this is at the checkout stand of the grocery store. Observe how quickly you say *I am fine* when asked how you are. See if you can allow yourself, even in these insignificant moments, to take time and come up with an answer that is authentic.

In the evening, take out your journal and write about your experiences today.

Lesson for Day Six

Nurturing Yourself

Imagine a world in which every woman gives to herself first what she gives first to others. She feeds herself first, she takes care of her body and finances first. She allows herself to receive. She would be teaching self love by example. Imagine what kind of gift this woman would be giving to her children and the world.

Before we move on to the next step in the Blossom Journey, I want to point out one more skill that you must allow yourself to learn. This skill dramatically improves your ability to be in touch with your heart. It is the skill of *self-nurturing*.

I know from my own life that the less we take care of our own needs and the less we nurture ourselves, then the less we have to give and the less we are able to love and be loved. When you are exhausted, it is much harder to feel connected to your body and to your real yes and no. To create a condition in which you operate optimally, meaning a place where you have the capacity to use all the tools shared in this book, like feeling your true yes and no and being able to hear and act on your intuition, you need sufficient sleep -and good food that nourishes your body. Having sufficient sleep and nourishing food are indispensable supports when it comes to feeling your true yes and no and being able to act on that felt sense.

You also need exercise, you need space to be by yourself, and you need time with friends, with family, and your intimate lover. It's not always the same all the time.

Sometimes you might need meat, some days your body just needs fruit. The key is to be tuned into your body, soul and spirit, honor whatever need you have, and act on it. Sometimes, especially when you are the mother of young children, it is extremely challenging to make the space to even consider your own needs.

I know I have gone too far when I start yelling at my children, when I am manifesting opposite behavior of who I have committed to being. I am committed to being love. Most of the women I work with make that commitment, too. They want all their relationships to be a reflection of that commitment.

EXERCISE

GIVING TO YOURSELF FIRST

Here is a very powerful tool for checking in to make sure you are giving to yourself first. (An analogy is that if you were a passenger seated on an airplane about to crash, unless you put on your oxygen mask first, you won't be able to help anyone else.) At any given time through your day, when you notice you are feeling uneasy or moody, take a few minutes and sit yourself down for a loving talk. Picture your inner child and ask her what she needs. Also ask if there is any other part of you that needs anything. Then come up with a plan that makes "everyone" happy.

BONUS

Connect to your inner child and come up with at least 10 ways you can give to yourself first. Start a "giving to myself first" journal or just write in your regular journal. Take a few minutes every day to note 3-5 things you did that day to give to yourself first. Literally go on a "giving to myself first" challenge.

LESSON
for Day Seven

WEEK THREE IN REVIEW

In this third week of the journey, you learned about all the different parts that make up you. You not only learned about them but more importantly you learned how to distinguish and honor them, so that you can move out of fragmentation into wholeness. You reconnected more and continued re-building the relationship with your wounded inner child. This part of you is starting to feel safer.

You learned that:

Your heart always knows what's good for you.

There is an innate intelligence that you have access to.

You can access this innate intelligence by knowing your true yes and no.

It is imperative to take time to check in with yourself, nurture yourself, and hear your own needs.

Step 4 on your Blossom Journey is called "See With Eyes of Truth." See with true eyes. Real–eyes. It's where you get to look at the truth of your affairs. This is where you go beyond just the parts of your psychological makeup and look at the bigger picture, the generational picture. All that makes up who you are.

EXERCISE

REFLECT BACK

Reflect back on Week Three of your Blossom Journey. Take out your journal and write your answers to these questions: *What was most helpful to you in this week's lessons? What kinds of shifts can you already see within yourself and in the beliefs you have been holding? What is starting to change in your life?*

Write what comes to you.

Week Four
SEE WITH EYES OF TRUTH

In the past three weeks, you have become more aware of your feelings and your feeling capacity. Last week you opened to your intuition, developing and strengthening your feeling capacity muscle even more. Because you are learning to feel again, you can "hear" your intuition and be able to access it as a safe guidance system. Your intuition will continue to be your guidance system on this journey and in life.

Weeks One through Four are structured in a way that makes you ready for the emotional integration work in Week Five. Look at it like this: If you had been training to run a 10K, Week Five is the day of the race. Before you actually participate in a race, you want to make sure you are in good shape. You do this by training the muscles you need, and in order to do the integration work next week, you need to be somewhat familiar with your feeling capacity and the concepts behind the integration process. Throughout the last three weeks and in this week, you are learning many different exercises that will help you.

Week Four is the midpoint of your Blossom Journey. But instead of it being the climax, meaning you went uphill until now and downhill from now on, look at your Blossom Journey as being more like an airport runway. The further you go, the more momentum you gain, until in Week Seven, you are ready to spread your wings to take off and fly.

Now that you know exactly how you can be connected to the voice of your heart and make different choices in your life, the necessary next step is to change your relationship with emotional pain. That's why this 4th step of the journey is all about seeing through the eyes of truth.

What is the truth behind your feeling of separation, your reactive behavior, or any act of unkindness? For most of us, it is our pain, our hurting heart, and our desire to make that go away. Wanting to make ourself feel better is at the root of all our relationship and life problems.

Lesson for Day One

SEEING PAIN IN A DIFFERENT LIGHT

Pain is a funny thing. It can hurt so much, yet it holds the key to all our freedom and healing. The problem that we, as Westerners, have with pain is that we see it as a bad thing, something to avoid. We look at pain as something that is our own, something personal, instead of seeing it in a broader context. We generally aren't aware that we carry pain for others.

When most of my clients first come to see me and are faced with their pain, their addictions, their relationship and life struggles, they think that what they are experiencing is uniquely theirs. They would give anything if they could just make this darn pain go away! And I don't blame them—what we feel in those moments of crisis can feel awful.

No one wants to be with their pain. When you look at almost any product or service that's offered in today's marketplace, you can see it is mostly geared towards distracting you from yourself; it is designed to help you make the pain go away. And I am not even talking medication here.

Look at, for instance, ice cream, or movies, or even fashion. You eat ice cream to feel better, you watch movies because you can't be with yourself or your partner, and you hunt the latest fashion to look and feel good.

Again, this is what I believe: We all come from a place of unconditional being before we incarnate into our bodies and are born. We, of course, expect that unconditional state to continue into this world. What we find instead is a place defined by conditions. There couldn't be a more conditional place in the universe than Planet Earth. Everything exists in the condition of duality. Black and white. Day and night. Peace and war. Opposites rule.

Now, I know I am getting somewhat esoteric and "out there," but these are the truths that I have found. Experiencing life and love conditionally creates your core pain. It usually creates a feeling of something being wrong with you. It creates the feeling of you and love being two separate things. In reality, the only thing that's wrong is your perception because at your core you and love are one.

This feeling of duality, of separation, is in all of us. And each of us comes up with our own mechanisms to sedate both this initial and subsequent experience of pain, so we can continue to live and not die from the pain (or so we think).

In reality, almost anyone on this planet has his or her own strategy to cope. Some become workaholics, others overeat or don't eat, smoke or drink, and yet others get addicted to relationship drama or sex.

THE TRUTH ABOUT ADDICTION

The truth about any addiction or unhealthy behavior is this: It's not a disease that you somehow attract out of the blue, but rather a deliberate mechanism to not feel the pain of the conditional, separate experience of being on earth.

It isn't your fault and it isn't your mother's fault. You come into this world not knowing what pain is, and as soon as it happens, as soon as the trauma or something else very painful happens to you, you invent something to not feel it, a strategy called a *sedation mechanism.*

How do you come up with this sedation mechanism? Well, you don't just come up with these pain-sedating mechanisms and strategies on your own; you subconsciously learn them from your family, your "tribe." Each individual soul seems to know: *This is how it's done in my family.*

I've seen so many times in my work that the way in which emotional pain is sedated in a family gets passed down from generation to generation. And not only that, but the pain is passed down, too. Children take on a lot for their parents, and even whole family systems, out of a kind of blind love.

No matter what face an addiction or drama puts on, they are all the same thing in disguise. They are an attempt at making pain go away. Such sedation mechanisms also don't belong only to one person, but are very often expressed by one person in the family who has subconsciously chosen to carry the pain for the entire family system.

The one with the trauma serves as a catalyst for all others. It may seem that that person has a lot of trauma and pain, and therefore is causing a lot of pain for the entire family, yet the truth is this soul, *you* for example, has taken on carrying all the pain, so the others don't have to feel it. All of this is happening beneath the surface, below the conscious level. It is the bottom of the iceberg that nobody ever sees until they ram into it.

This is a very different way to look at pain and your love predicament. This way of looking at pain, and seeing it for what it really is, was what single-handedly made it possible for me to integrate my core wounds. *Family Constellation work* was what brought this way of looking at pain into my life.

Even though next week is dedicated to learning about the integration tools in depth and how to use them, this week is a good time to start learning about Family Constellation work.

What I love most about Family Constellations is that it is not a theoretic modality that some academic doctor came up with. Rather, it is a process that was used by indigenous people for many generations and then observed by a Westerner who happened to have had some background in family therapy (or so the story goes).

That person's name is Bert Hellinger, the father of what's known today as *phenomenological psychotherapy*. Phenomenological psychotherapy is an approach that was developed out of observation of phenomena, things that occur on their own without any human doing. Beginning in the 1930s, several therapists, including social worker Virginia Satyr and psychiatrist Jakob Moreno, started seeing the individual client in the context of a family system rather than as an isolated person. Out of their work, the systemic approach to psychotherapy developed.

Hellinger fell in love with this systemic approach, and by working with it extensively, he began observing certain recurring, age-old, hidden "Orders of Love" that operate in the depths of family organisms, which became the spine of the Family Constellation work. (We will discuss these orders next week in depth.)

Most of the modalities I was learning seemed to have some inherent possibility of client manipulation; they all seemed to leave room for interpretation by the therapist, which meant that the client didn't necessarily get the truth. I was only interested in finding modalities that worked with truth rather than with the opinion of the therapist. Family Constellation work, if it is done right, is the only modality that is waterproof against the therapist's conscious or unconscious manipulative influences.

Clients, when working with a therapist, are in an extremely vulnerable position. They come to the therapist placing their lives somewhat in their hands. Working phenomenally rules out any power I have over my client. Working phenomenally means that you work with what is shown by the process itself, visible to any outside bystander and not just to the therapist. This approach completely shifts the therapist/client dynamic to that of equals, observing together an unfolding process.

Traditional therapy makes room to talk about old pain and tries to teach new behaviors to avoid future pain. Some forms also encourage you to express your pain, and some might even teach how to access and allow emotions. But none of the traditional modalities I know of are geared towards teaching how you can allow your feelings and process them in a way that helps them integrate. Also, none of them address the whole system but rather look only at the individual, you, thereby missing 90% of what's really going on. It's similar to our "modern" approach to health. Instead of looking at the body as a whole organism which functions best when all parts are working well together, doctors isolate and treat a symptom as if it were not connected to everything else that's going on.

The point I want to make today is that it is important to "see" the truth that you are much more connected to your family system and ancestry than you think you are. You are a part of something much grander and that each family has its own unique way of coping with pain. What you carry is not just your own trauma but a systemic pain from other souls in your family lineage. Through Constellation work it becomes very clear just how powerful this unconscious connection to our family lineage is.

Tomorrow you will learn exactly how Constellation work is done.

EXERCISE

PATTERNS OF INHERITED PAIN

Take out your journal and reflect on the statement: "This is how it is done in my family." See if you can come up with 3-5 pain sedation mechanisms that you "inherited" from your tribe. You can go back to Week Two, when we looked at what you do to keep yourself a small pond, to jog your memory. See if you can identify patterns. Write about your discoveries.

Lesson for Day Two

THERE IS SO MUCH MORE TO LIFE THAN YOU CAN SEE

How can you know that there is so much more to life than you can see?

Family Constellation work shows this to anyone who watches. I promised you yesterday that you would find out exactly how a Constellation is done. In addition to that, we will go deeper with the theme of "seeing the truth" and find out more about how it is you can access these unseen forces.

Traditionally, Family Constellations were only done in group settings. Today there are many versions of the original process, as almost every facilitator has added his or her wisdom and additional background to it. It can be done one-on-one and even over the phone. I have developed my own way of working with single clients with Constellations called "Soul Motions." I have seen group Constellations that were very effective and some that were ineffective. I have also seen one-on-one Constellations that were very effective and some that were not. It all depends on the skill level of the facilitator and the readiness of the client to do the work.

I will describe the process from a group setting perspective. The only disadvantage that people sometimes see in group work is that they have to become "naked" in front of others which can feel uncomfortable. From a therapeutic perspective, allowing yourself to become vulnerable in front of other human beings can be healing in and of itself, but people should still have the choice, and I do respect personal preferences.

When done in a group, this is what a Constellation looks like. Let's say it is your Constellation.

To begin, you and the facilitator, the one who is leading the Constellation, would have a conversation in private before the group actually meets. During that conversation, the facilitator asks you to relate what your issues or blocks are.

He or she also asks you if there were any tragedies, early deaths, unborn children, acts of crime, etc. in your family that you know of. Not just in your immediate family but as far back as you can remember. The facilitator is not so much interested in hearing all the stories of personal drama that are going on between family members, but only true facts such as your father's mother died when he was two or your grandfather was killed in the war. Based on the information the facilitator receives from you and based on the Orders of Love, the facilitator will have a sense of which people it would be beneficial to have represented in your Constellation .

Generally, the work is done with only one side of the family at a time. For example, I wouldn't work with your father's side of the family at the same time as with your mother's side, or, if you are married, your side and your husband's.

There are several forms a Constellation can take. Some Constellations involve your family members, some might involve parts of yourself, others involve greater universal concepts like you and God or you and life. Still others might involve you alone but at different times in your life. And there are several other forms that I am not mentioning here. The most traditional forms, and in my opinion the most profound ones, especially when you are first starting, are the classical

Family Constellations. From what I have seen and experienced, the family is our root, our base. After we have done some groundwork, we can expand and experiment and gain insight into other aspects of ourselves.

Let's say the issue you want to work on is healing your broken heart. Let's just assume for example's sake that I am your facilitator, and in our private conversation you told me that there are no tragedies on your mother's side, but your father's mother died when your father was four years old. I don't know the reasons why, nor do I want to know why, unlike in other therapy modalities.

The other group participants don't know anything about you. They only know what you state your issue is. They know that you want to work on healing your broken heart.

When a Constellation is "set up," we always try to start as small as possible. After you state your issue to the group, which generally consists of 15-20 people, I then check in with you about how you are doing. When you are ready, I tell you who needs to be represented in your Constellation. We need someone to represent you, someone to represent your father, and someone to represent your mother. In a Constellation, other people from the group are asked to represent the members of your family or the parts that are needed in a Constellation. Your physical relatives aren't actually in the room.

People who stand in for your family members are called *representatives,* because that is what they do—they represent those people or parts, rather than *play* them, as in a role play. This is a crucial distinction of Constellation work and the reason it is phenomenological. If a person were to play your mother, they would act out of their own interpretation and most likely mix their story in with yours. When people represent, as opposed to play, they are simply asked to pay attention to phenomena that occur in their bodies and souls, which leaves very little room for their ego and story to become involved.

Next, you choose the people in the group who will represent you and your family members. You get up from your chair and intuitively approach whomever feels right for representing you, your mother, or your father. You stand in front of them, look them in the eye, and ask them if they are willing to represent your mother, father, and you. When someone has agreed to represent, he or she will also get up from the chair and stand and wait in a designated area until you have picked all representatives; they then stand in a row.

Your next step is to set up the representatives into an actual Constellation; this is why the work received its name, as a constellation is a specific organization of elements. To begin, you place all representatives, one after the other, in different locations in the room. You do this by stepping behind each one of them, closing your eyes, holding on to their shoulders, and letting your body intuitively guide you and them to a place that feels right in the room. You might place the representative for yourself on the outside looking in, your father on the opposite side looking away, and your mother in between the two of you. Next you take a seat, and all you have to do from that point on is sit and watch what unfolds.

What unfolds is often times unbelievable, almost magical, and very hard to describe in words. This is where the phenomenon takes over and the truth about your issue is most often revealed. The "strangers" that you picked to represent your family, just by means of you placing them in certain locations and relationships in the room, and by feeling what is physically and emotionally going on within them, seem to know the truth of your issue.

What Hellinger observed over and over again in doing this process was that illness or disease develops in a system when the love that wants to flow naturally between all the members, whether it is within a family and organization or one person, can't flow.

A Constellation naturally starts out showing the state where love doesn't flow and ideally ends up in a state where the love between the different elements, people and family members flows again. This resurrected flow in Constellation terms is called the *resolution*. Basically it can be said that when love is flowing, there is peace.

All our issues are essentially a variation on the same theme, *I don't have love and I need love.*

Generally, a Constellation takes about 45 minutes from start to resolution. During that time, the client watches their representatives move, which changes the dynamic; they will also say certain things and the facilitator will guide them to state "healing sentences" to each other. Often times the Constellation itself will ask for things, like people being added or taken out. Shifts begin to happen within the client by simply observing what is happening, by paying close attention to the phenomenon.

Let's take our example of your father looking in a specific direction and wanting to stay focused there. As an observer, a reasonable question to ask is, what or who is he looking at rather than looking at your mother and you? Based on what you told me before the Constellation, I know your father lost his mother at a young age. I will bring a representative in for his mother and see if he has a reaction to it. The representative doesn't know who I am placing across from him, because you and I talked before meeting with the group. One scenario could be that the father's representative, when faced with your father's mother's representative, would fall on his knees and start sobbing.

Such movement is a sign that in order for you to find resolution, your father has to be able to reconnect with his mother, whom he is still missing. This missing makes your father unable to look at you, or in other words, to be present for you. You, in turn, were longing for your father's love all your life and weren't getting it. Your soul, knowing about the state of your father's soul, broke your heart. The pain you were feeling was not only the pain of yearning for your father's love, but also the pain of his broken heart, caused by his early loss.

In your relationships with men, you were unconsciously looking for your father's love. Your lovers pick this longing up unconsciously as well, and it pushes them energetically away, because on a soul level they know they can never replace your father's love. In a way, what you are unconsciously asking of them is too much. Only when you get your father's love from your father are you free to receive the appropriate kind of love from your lover. Only when you are receiving your father's love will the love that you receive from a lover satisfy your heart.

This is a very simplified explanation of what might be the cause of your hurting heart and your relationship dilemma. But more important than finding out the cause is the actual emotional integration that is happening within you while you are watching the Constellation and the resolution.

Constellations are so powerful because you get to connect with the truth of your emotional imprints. You get to feel what's in your trash can, so to speak. Often representatives feel it for you, and they can help you to move it out and through your system by letting the energy go through their own system. No talk is necessary, no mind, no analyzing. The only thing necessary is you seeing the truth about yourself and your family, your loved ones, and authentically connecting with your feelings.

THE KNOWING FIELD

As mentioned before, what I know today, because of my work with Family Constellations, is that we are surrounded and influenced by people and events we have no conscious awareness of. How is it that total strangers, who don't know anything about us, when placed in a Constellation as representatives, know so much? This is a very good question, and not one a skeptical mind or a mind that hasn't experienced Constellation work can answer. Even people who've worked with Constellations for a long time don't really know the answer.

From what I've experienced over and over again, there seems to be some kind of "field" that exists to connect us all in life. For lack of a better word, in Constellation Circles this is called the *Knowing Field*, a benevolent, non-judgmental, energetic space that is like a big memory. It contains the knowledge of what you need to know and integrate in order to evolve to the next step in your journey towards wholeness and love. The Knowing Field is what the Constellation facilitator relies on when guiding a client through a Constellation, and it requires him or her to be completely present.

The Knowing Field is not connected to a personal or ego level, but rather to an essential soul level in each one of us, providing a web of knowledge that unifies us all. It does not show up in a person's fantasies or opinions – it can only be observed when paying close attention to what is actually happening in a Constellation in any given moment. As an energetic field, it can only be accessed through the body, through sensing and feeling.

First time representatives often feel insecure as to how to "play" the role. As mentioned earlier, because we work with the Knowing Field, no playing is required, only being present. A facilitator will ask you about your physical reactions and feelings when you are being a representative; all that is required from you as a representative is that you honestly feel what's going on in your body and that you give account of that.

EXERCISE

DISCOVER YOUR ROOTS

Begin to discover your roots. Go to www.BlossomBook.com/ supplements and download a template of a genealogy tree. This is a map of your family history. Fill in the details to make it your own. Find out who the people were that lived before you and how they may have more influence on your current issues than you have been aware of.

LESSON
for Day Three

AWARENESS IS ALL IT TAKES

You might think of your relationship troubles or your trauma as the cause of your agony, but as discussed, your trauma is partly the result of love becoming *entangled* somewhere down the line, most likely in your family's system.

The word *entanglement* is key to this understanding. Think of a ball of yarn that has a lot of knots, making it useless for knitting. It can't perform its proper function unless you take the time and patience to sit down and follow the thread to untie the knots. Now, we human beings are obviously no ball of yarn. But we still become entangled.

An entanglement in human terms is when someone can't perform their proper function, when they cannot be themselves, because they became involved or knotted up in other people's fate. This happens on a soul or energetic level—you don't physically do it—and you don't do it with random strangers, but with those closest to you, those that you love the most. You get entangled with them out of love.

Let me give you a real life example from my life: You may recall my story of how my grandmother was in a prison camp after World War II from the age of 11 until 20. She was starving and in a lot of despair during that time of her life. Interestingly, I starved myself from 11 years old until I was 20, dealing with the eating disorders of bulimia and anorexia. I was entangled with my grandmother. On a subconscious level, I thought that by me aligning with her fate and undergoing what she went through, I could ease her pain.

I teach my clients to look at their family as a kind of mobile, the hanging decoration, on which every person has his or her place. If one person is excluded as the black sheep or because they did a "bad" deed or because something so painful happened to them that it was brushed under the carpet, then an imbalance occurs in the hanging mobile and it tips over to one side. An unspoken law in the energetic world is that imbalance in a system cannot be tolerated. What happens then is that someone from the next generation steps into that place to restore balance.

In my case, I had taken on my grandmother's fate, so what she endured would not be forgotten or brushed under the rug in my family. Again, this is all about love, and love doesn't tolerate exclusion. Love will make sure to find a way to include everything and everyone.

To bring this thought to completion, the taking on of someone else's place, like I did with my grandmother, is what is meant by *entanglement*. My soul somehow got knotted up with hers, which didn't allow me to be fully myself. Instead, I was living out someone else's fate. Her fate. I was not happy.

I feel very fortunate to be living in the time we are living in, because you and I are at a point in human consciousness where we are aware of and can transform these entanglements, creating a paradise on earth. Up until now, pain was passed on unconsciously from generation to generation. Parents raised their children as their parents did. Granted, each generation rebelled a bit against the older generations, but the gap between the generations was never resolved. In an attempt to do it better than our parents, we overcompensate and still aren't any closer to our own children than we were with our own mother—or if we don't have a child, we are not close with our mother but are becoming more and more just like her.

We are so blessed because you and I are the first generation to have several tools at our disposal that help to make the unconscious visible. Family Constellations is one of these tools. This means that we are the ones who can bring real change to our entire family system and the generations to come. Through Family Constellation work we can break the chains of unconscious patterns by resolving those generational issues once and for all.

I tell my clients that whatever you can see, you can change. Whatever you can see with eyes of truth, whatever you can *real-eyes*, meaning "realize" (a word play my spiritual teacher, Michael Brown, came up with), you can change. Awareness is the first step to change. Family Constellation work shows the truth of your issues, and because it is a process you watch and are fully present for, it helps you to integrate those generational core wounds. By seeing the truth unfold before you, you are giving your nervous system a new emotional imprint, replacing pain with resolution.

The integration of emotional pain is not a difficult experience, it is a freeing one, and there is no need to be afraid. Through the work you are doing now, you are not only freeing yourself, you are also setting your children free and all the generations in your family to come.

Awareness is all it takes to break the chain of destructive behaviors that are passed on from generation to generation.

Let me give you another example: As I mentioned earlier, my mother was physically and emotionally abused as a child by her alcoholic father and by a mother who didn't stand up for her. My mother did everything in her conscious power to prevent my siblings and me from having the same upbringing, and we didn't. My parents both raised us in an anti-authoritarian, loving environment. Nevertheless, my mom didn't protect me. In an attempt to give me the freedom she never had, she gave me too much freedom, and I was left hanging with no real support from her.

We grew further and further apart. The systemic pain did not get healed. Yes, I had a much better childhood than either of my parents had, but the core pain of feeling disconnected and not connected in love with my parents, just as they had experienced with their parents, dominated my life and all my intimate relationships.

I come across this same dynamic often. Mothers tell me that because of their own history, they tried to do everything to protect their daughters, but somehow they couldn't. Daughters tell me that their moms thought they protected them and gave them everything they needed, but the reality in all of these cases is that the mothers fail to truly *see* their daughters. They often push their daughters away by suffocating them with too much "love," too much protection. They fail to see the states their daughters are in, because as mothers they haven't integrated their own trauma. The subconscious mind, still unintegrated, is stronger than any intellectual knowing they have about their own history. As long as their trauma hasn't fully come into awareness and become integrated, the subconscious protection mechanism is going to override all else.

If there are unresolved entanglements, mother and daughter are literally living in different realities, even though they think they share the same one.

As you've already learned, your parents are your first loves, and your first experiences of blissful oneness and painful separation. And while eventually you must separate and go your own way, you still carry your parents in your heart.

Again, you are here to grow and your parents are your greatest teachers. When you can be around them and enjoy their company, truly feeling the love they have for you and you for them, you will be capable of having relationship experiences far beyond the limited kinds you have been used to in your life.

The tools you will be learning over the course of the next few weeks are all about helping you to integrate your core pain. They are about opening your heart through integrating your first experiences of love and pain (again, everyone intermingles the two and gets them mixed up), and redefining them, so you can grow beyond a limited experience of love into the full bloom of an open-hearted, intimate, complete relationship with yourself, others and the world.

EXERCISE

EXPLORING YOUR PAIN

Take out your journal and reflect on the question: What pain have you taken on and from whom? Journal about your discoveries.

LESSON
for Day Four

HOW PAIN SERVES US

Pain is the thing that nudges us to keep growing. The old saying "no pain, no gain" is true even if traditionally it means that unless you put a ton of sweat and tears into something, like learning how to play the violin or training to be a world-class athlete, you won't succeed. I mean it not in the sense of putting so much effort into something, but because encountering painful experiences is inherent to the growth process. You grow because you are in pain, and you want the pain to change. The "gain" is the *you* that you grow into being, because of the pain.

Truly, if there was no pain, we wouldn't need to change or grow. This is one of the basic principles of the Blossom Journey, and that is why I've mentioned it frequently in this book. This mind shift is so important for you to make. The pain, in and of itself, is not what kills you, even though it may seem to be the case. What is killing you is your resistance to the pain.

The resistance plays out in you wanting your life to be different. Wanting to make your mother and father happy, to change them. Wanting to fulfill your mother's dream of having a perfect life and being the perfect one. The resistance comes from your own feeling of entitlement to "a good life." The resistance to what is, is what creates our suffering. In the first days of this journey, you learned about *feeling it to heal it*. The next few days are when the rubber meets the road. As long as you are suffering, you are not really feeling the pain, but rather resisting feeling it. You think you feel it, and then you go into your head and leave your body. You create stories about it, start looking for ways out, for reasons, for justifications, and so on.

I am not saying that you are not entitled to a good life and love; I believe that we all are. But a good life isn't a life in which you just lay on the beach and cruise through. A good life is life with all its up and downs. A good life is a life where you are able to be the container, allow all emotions, and let the waves ride through you without lashing out because you hurt so much. When you become aware enough to stop being reactive and instead learn to ride the waves, you stop creating more pain for everyone involved. Then you can feel the truth that your life is a good life, as it is.

When we look at the world around us, we see pain everywhere. There is war, family drama and crime in many places. Knowing this, how come the number one thing we try to avoid is the number one thing that is prevalent in the world?

My explanation for this phenomenon is that *what we resist, persists*. So many people are currently resisting feeling their pain (or any so-called negative emotion), that they are unintentionally creating more. The more you want something to go away, and struggle with it just being there, the more energy and attention you give to it. You feed it the power it needs to survive.

In reality, it is not the pain itself that persists in making you feel bad—it is your resistance to it. Pain is an intense feeling, but when you allow yourself to feel it, it doesn't stay but moves through and transforms you. It is one of the bigger waves in the ocean. The resistance to pain, on the other hand, feels never-ending, doesn't move, and keeps you in a state of suffering. It's the equivalent of you trying to stop a tsunami—it will always win. Wherever you are right now, whether you are feeling your pain or you are feeling nothing, whether you are horrified by it or not, there are ways to get in touch with it all, ways to transform it, ways that will not kill you , but will help to heal you.

The pain will not kill you. But your resistance and the condition that results from it just might. I am aware that I'm repeating myself here, but it is so important, and that is why I am stating it over and over again. The only thing that really helps in transforming pain is to feel it, to allow it, and to digest it. Period!

EXERCISE

WRITE ABOUT YOUR PAIN

Take out pen and paper and write a letter to yourself. Take some time and think about who you have become because of your pain. Write about yourself as if you were looking back at your life, witnessing it all along, and describe the woman that you see. Write as if you were writing a letter about this person (you), as if she was your best friend, and you are writing about her to her. ("Dear Carolin, I've been watching you and your pain your whole life....."). Give lots of examples of how your pain has shaped you and led to life choices you've made.

BONUS

Put this letter in a self addressed envelope and then email me for an address to send to you. My email is: Carolin@Carolin-Hauser.com. In the near future, you can expect to get a little surprise in the mail when I send it back to you.

LESSON for Day Five

YOUR BODY IS THE DOORWAY TO LIFE

We have touched upon how your body is the doorway to life throughout the Blossom Journey, especially in regards to your feelings and your feeling capacity. Now, I know this is easier said than done. I used to be the master at *not feeling*. I thought I had feelings, but I didn't really—none that I would allow myself to actually experience. I was only able to *think* I felt something. I never allowed myself to feel anything. I thought that feeling would be too painful. Because of this block, I was living entirely in my head. I did not inhabit my body for fear of having feelings.

Your body is what connects you to life, to the present moment, to reality. Your head is where you reside when it gets too uncomfortable in your body. Your body is where you feel. Your feeling capacity is all in your body, so if the feelings get too intense, you slowly, bit by bit, leave it—that's only logical. The result, though, is that you feel empty, like a shell with nothing in it. And the reality is *you are empty*. Your body, which is your only vehicle to experience life, is empty of your awareness.

To only inhabit the mental part of your body means that you are trapped in a painful past or a wishful future, and you never actually are present in the now moment. Your mind creates a prison built out of time.

Time is a mental construct, not a *real* one. In eternity and truth, time doesn't exist or even matter. (Here on earth it does—don't get me wrong!) In reality, there always is only this very moment. And in this very moment, everything is always well.

Time is a construct and you as a human being need time to orient yourself to it. Time gives you a sense of direction, from here to there. Time in and of itself is neither good nor bad. It simply is a navigational tool. Unfortunately, time, when you cling to your past or future, becomes a prison that blocks you from experiencing the aliveness of the present moment.

It leaves you with a feeling of waiting. Waiting to have love and intimacy, waiting to have the life that you want, waiting to feel fully present in your life. As soon as you are here now, fear dissipates, because fear is generated by the mind when it is fixated on past experiences and false predictions.

Fear makes you close down, causing you to feel empty, disconnected and alone. But when fear disappears, you open. To be open means to be love. Love in human form is the experience of an open heart. This can only happen in the present moment. It can only happen when you step out of your habitual mind and into your feeling body and heart.

Again, the Blossom Journey is all about learning ways to move out of your head into your heart, out of separation into connectedness. Out of the prison of time into present moment awareness.

My client Judith told me about her inability to sleep at night. Night after night, she lay awake looking at the clock on her nightstand and being tortured by the slow passing of time. A minute seemed like an eternity to her. She remembered the days when she was a child immersed in play, art, or whatever she was doing, and how time just flew by.

Judith couldn't understand what had happened. Why had she become so disengaged from everything? Nothing seemed to be able to hold her attention or interest. She was unable to stop listening to the constant discussion in her head about her awful, lonely life. She wished she could go back in time and be an innocent child again. But what she really was asking me was this: *How can I become present in my life again?*

Looking back, I can see what had happened to me during my toilet wake-up moment. For the first time, I was re-entering my body (after having entered it as a newborn), and time stood still—it was a timeless moment. Today, I know that whenever I lose track of time, I am present in my life.

In those kinds of moments, you just *are*. You aren't thinking or *doing* life, you are *being* life. We all have had these moments. We had them maybe while dancing or listening to a story or watching a child play or a butterfly move effortlessly from flower to flower.

EXERCISE

ATTENDING TO THE NOW MOMENT

Take out your journal and reflect on your moments of connectedness. Throughout your day pay attention to whether you are in your head (thinking about the past and worrying about something or planning the future) or in your body, in the now moment. Again, you know that you are in the now moment when time just flies and you lose track of it.

LESSON for Day Six

INTEGRITY

You might have noticed that I have a real love for language and the written word, and that I love to play with words. The word *integration* comes from the word *integrity*. At first glance, you might think that one has nothing to do with the other.

The dictionary states that one of the meanings of *integration* is "a coordination of mental processes into a normal, effective personality or with the individual's environment." A definition for *integrity* is "the firm adherence to a code of especially moral values, the quality or state of being undivided, an unimpaired condition." When you look at the root for both in Latin, you end up with "integer," which means wholeness. I love this.

What I have observed in my clients and myself is that when we are integrated, when we move from fragmentation into wholeness by doing the integration work, everything we do in life has more integrity, or wholeness. And that's not because we are all of a sudden more able to stick to the rules of a moral code. It's because we are able to keep our heart open and feel our feelings. We feel the consequences of our actions and words, because we are present.

For example, during the days I suffered from bulimia, I was very un-integrated, meaning I was in a lot of soul pain, and I did a lot of things that were "immoral." The stuff I would do in order to consume food was unbelievable. My husband always shakes his head when I tell him the stories about me during that time, he can hardly believe they are true.

For example, I'd offer to babysit my friend's children at night, just so I could raid their refrigerators. I would steal money from the people I was working for to pay for my expensive addiction to food, and I would do almost everything a heroin addict does to get my drug. And of course I would lie. I lied so much.

As you can see, these are things that had no integrity at all. But the more I integrated my pain using the tools you are learning right now, the less I would do these outrageous things. I was more and more connected to myself and my heart, and therefore to others.

YOU ARE BEING INITIATED

Before we move on to learning more about how you can integrate your pain, I want to share with you one more thing. You are being initiated right now. You are initiating yourself.

In ancient times, only a few had the privilege of going through any kind of initiation process. It was believed that the common people needed guidance and weren't able to access God directly. This went on for a very long time in the history of human kind. As you probably know, many tribal cultures had initiation rituals for boys and girls when crossing over from childhood into adulthood.

I believe that right now we are all experiencing a sort of initiation like that, even though it may not be marked outwardly with a ceremony.

In mythology, initiation is often depicted as the soul burning up in flames, such as the phoenix rising from the ashes. Transforming and integrating your pain is like going through the fire, a fire that burns deeply in your soul. You come out transformed at the other end, opened and thankful, knowing that all is well. You know that life will always remain a great mystery, but you are certain that your purpose is to express and experience unconditional love this time around. In the end, nothing else matters.

It is an honor and a blessing that you can experience and facilitate your very own initiation in the times we are in right now. We are at the cutting edge of consciousness, and you are a pioneer. You are paving the way for a more enlightened and more loving new earth through your personal growth and relationship work.

One woman at a time, one heart at a time—you are doing it.

You are it!

Along with experiencing your very own initiation goes the realization that up until now you have been chasing happiness. Happiness is a concept that contains the notion that if and when such and such happens, you will be happy. Happiness is always a very temporary state. Yes, you are happy when your husband or lover remembers your birthday or brings you flowers, but for how many minutes does this happiness last?

You might have waited for the flowers thinking that then you would be happy, only to discover one day after you finally get them, you still feel as empty as before.

Initiation reveals that when you are looking for happiness, you'll always be on the hunt and never get there. It will also reveal the greater peace of true joy.

Joy is a state of being that is not based on an "if, then or when" scenario. Joy always is. Just like love. Just like your true being. The more you can get out of the way, meaning the more you travel from your head into your heart, the more you can be in joy. The heart is the organ that rejoices. An open heart flows between joy, peace, sadness, being touched, being moved, and so on.

EXERCISE

LETTING GO

Today I invite you to create a sacred ritual for yourself. Find rocks or pieces of paper on which you write all the things that you are shedding, letting go of right now, to evolve as a new you. This would include all of the pain you've been holding on to, your attachment to things being permanent or necessary for your happiness. Write any generational pain you've discovered. Practice letting all of this go.

After writing down all that you are releasing, you can either burn the paper or toss the rocks in a river or lake. Consciously allow yourself to give away this "load" to the universe.

LESSON for Day Seven

WEEK FOUR IN REVIEW

This week, you learned how pain serves you, that it is the thing that nudges you and makes you grow. It's not only about what you have experienced, but also what those who came before you experienced. You carry stuff that has been passed down from many generations.

You learned that:

> *What you are truly feeling is the resistance to pain; pain in and of itself is neither good nor bad but only an intense emotion.*

> *Out of love we all, as children, take on stuff from our parents and ancestors.*

> *You belong to a whole system and carry a lot of pain for others.*

> *Awareness is all it takes and Family Constellation work is one of the few processes that makes the subconscious visible.*

> *You are going through your own initiation.*

Now that you have learned to look at pain in a new way, it is time to learn all about how you can transform it. Integrating your pain will enable you to see whatever is coming toward you in life for what it is. In your everyday life, this means that what drove you crazy about your partner before will no longer drive you crazy, and that which hurt you so much before and caused you to shut down will no longer have this effect.

Instead of leading your life through the experiences of a hurt two-year old, you will grow up to become the radiant, full woman you have always wanted to be. Fully inhabiting your life in this way, you are capable of having emotionally, spiritually, intellectually, energetically and sexually fulfilling relationships and the life of your dreams.

EXERCISE

REFLECT BACK

Reflect back on Week Four of your Blossom Journey. Take out your journal and write your answers to these questions: *What was most helpful to you in this week's lessons? What kinds of shifts can you already see within yourself and in the beliefs you have been holding? What is starting to change in your life?*

Write what comes to you.

Week Five
STRETCH BEYOND YOUR LIMITS

Step 5 of the Blossom Journey is for you to stretch yourself beyond your limits. This week you will be introduced to the "how to" of emotional integration.

Integration is work. But it's worth every ounce of sweat and tears. And yes, there might be tears, but not the ones that will drown you. I promise that you will only be given what you can take. In a funny way, life works that way.

You've learned how Family Constellation work is a great process for integration. But you need a facilitator to use this tool. All along in my practice, I was on the lookout for a tool that would enable my clients to integrate without needing an outside helper, because I am a big advocate of self-help. I'd rather teach someone how to fish than give someone a fish. There are times when it is absolutely useful to have someone help you, to have someone take you by the hand, to have someone that can help you remove your bigger blocks; but it's great to have a tool that lets you deal with the smaller stuff yourself.

A few years back when I started remembering my own early sexual abuse, I wasn't able to find anyone to facilitate a Constellation for me, which left me in desperate need of finding my own solution. Help came in the form of a book called *The Presence Process*, by Michael Brown. I love and adore this man, who has been a great influence on the way I work. The focus of his process is the integration of emotional imprints without outside help. The main tool that Michael teaches is called Consciously Connected Breathing.

LESSON
for Day One

CONSCIOUSLY CONNECTED BREATHING

Consciously Connected Breathing is a breathing technique that models the way that we breathe naturally as children. As children we don't breathe in, take a break and then breathe out. We breathe in and out as a continuous airflow without breaks in between. As children we do this automatically. As adults, we have to consciously connect our breathing because we breathe in, pause and breathe out. This is why it is called Consciously Connected Breathing. We consciously have to connect our in and out breath.

Let's look at why Consciously Connected Breathing helps integrate the same way as Family Constellations work.

When trauma happens, energy gets stuck in the nervous system (again, you will learn more about the nervous system next week). This energy can only get unstuck through our unconditional feelinging it. This is what is happening when we watch a Constellation. When we breathe in a consciously connected way, this is what happens also.

As mentioned, in order for you to integrate, you have to feel your stuck emotions—in other words, you have to be able to open the lid of the trash can without being swept away or paralyzed by fear. Presence helps us to do that. Breath helps us to be present. Breath happens in the body. Presence only takes place in your body. Most of us, as you have learned, don't inhabit the body from the shoulders downward anymore. We found

193

comfortable shelter in the space between our ears and the stories that we keep telling ourselves about life and truth. Think about it—if you didn't have a body, how would you exist on this earthly plane?

Maybe as an angel, but not as a human being.

As a human being, you require a body. Anything real can only be experienced through the body. The breath brings you back into your physicality. Through Consciously Connected Breathing, you focus your complete attention on yourself. In other words, you completely and unconditionally pay attention to what is happening inside of you. Instead of only paying attention to what is happening in your mind, like listening to or being trapped by your thoughts, you enter into the realm of feeling and sensing, using your feeling capacity.

I teach the Consciously Connected Breathing technique as the main integration tool for everyday life. I recommend to my clients that whenever they are triggered and can catch themselves, that they sit, close their eyes, just sense the emotion and breathe through it.

I recommend Family Constellations to my clients whenever they encounter a major issue or block that doesn't seem to go away, no matter how hard they try to breathe through it and integrate on their own. You know you are encountering a subconscious block when, despite all of your efforts, you are unable to change, and the same situation keeps showing up again and again. That time is the perfect time for a Family Constellation.

Exercise

Consciously Connected Breathing

Rather than explaining how the Consciously Connected Breathing is done, I recorded a 15 minute example session for you that you can follow along with. Listen to the recording of a Consciously Connected Breathing session at: www.BlossomBook.com/recordings

Moving forward over the next 21 days, practice the Consciously Connected Breathing technique for 15 minutes every day. It takes 21 repetitions to form a new habit. During and after you are done with the 21 days, use this tool to integrate your imprints whenever you are triggered.

LESSON
for Day Two

THE ILLUSION OF INDEPENDENCE

While your focus of this week is to practice the Consciously Connected Breathing technique and start to feel your emotional imprints and integrate them, there is so much I want to share with you that I have learned from my work with Family Constellations. All my clients have found that learning these insights has helped them greatly on their journey. Most of the teaching points compiled in this week's material came in response to questions that clients have asked me on this journey. They wanted to know exactly how Family Constellations and sexual trauma integration are connected.

As mentioned last week, first and foremost, working with and experiencing the Knowing Field has taught me that there is so much more to life than we are ever able to comprehend. This was part of the reason why, when I was sharing my story in Part I, I took the detour to go so far back in my own history. Family Constellations has shown me over and over again that the people who have lived before us are still with us today, they are still around us, and they are forces you can call upon. Ancient people, like Native American tribes, still live with that knowledge, because they haven't felt the need to individuate to the degree of most modern societies.

One can say that obviously it is necessary for humanity to individuate to a degree where we feel completely isolated, otherwise it wouldn't be happening, but I personally think that we had to go so far in one direction to come back again to a healthier middle path. If we hadn't gone through feeling like we didn't need anyone, we wouldn't have been able to come to the realization that we are *inter*dependent beings, meaning independent but dependent at the same time, and we would still be fighting for our independence against each other.

I think we are still caught in the in between stage of wanting to be independent and realizing that we are *inter*dependent. We are still defining and finding out for ourselves what that means.

I want to give you an example of several situations where the Constellation process revealed something traditional therapy would never have been able to.

Several clients have come to see me with the same issue: they felt like they were missing a part of themselves. They were looking for this missing part as "the One" in all their boyfriends and lovers, but the longing would never subside. All of them were constantly beating themselves up for having this longing to merge with another. They felt like they were somehow faulty, because they just couldn't cope with being on their own. To compensate, they learned to be emotionally independent and acquired the skill of being able to have casual sex and casual relationships.

Many of them had learned from therapists and self-help seminars that their problem was low self esteem and a lack of self-love. When they came to me, they seemed strong and independent, knowing exactly what they wanted in life and what they didn't want. They had gotten the idea that their independence and ability to create a "successful life" was the equal of self-love and that it meant they didn't need a lover. The truth is their longing didn't go away, and they came to me because they wanted to find out why.

In all of these cases, we did a Constellation around the issue of "the missing part."

When we started the Constellation, we didn't know what the resolution would be, but in all of the Constellations, what showed up was that the mothers of these women had all conceived twins. The Constellations also showed that these twin siblings vanished before birth. I did some research into the phenomenon of vanishing twins after this happened and found out that indeed 85 percent of pregnancies start out with twin fetuses.

In the Constellations, my clients got a chance to reconnect with their twin siblings, and they finally found the cause for their longing. They found out that it wasn't just some psychological deficiency that made them long so deeply for a missing part; no, they truly were missing a sibling. As a result, they were able to give their twin a place in their heart and their life. They can feel him or her around them and have stopped searching for their missing part in another.

My clients who had this experience learned that all their feelings are valid, even if those feelings are not explainable to our logical mind. In their conscious minds, they didn't know they had a sibling, but their soul and subconscious mind did, because they had shared room with him or her in their mother's womb and probably before. I am saying *before* because when my son was about to be born, my daughter at age four said to me, "Mama, I know what he looks like. He has hair like me and the same big smile. We are twins, but when we got ready to come down from heaven's meadow, he got scared and sent me first." When my son was born, he looked almost identical to my daughter. It made me think of the possibility that siblings are together even before they are born.

But back to my clients. The knowledge that we are connected to so much more and the direct experience of this truth gave the women I was seeing a tremendous sense of peace. They now know that there is nothing wrong with them. Their longing now has a home, and their lovers don't have to fulfill an impossible need. Seeking the love of a sibling from a partner only pushes that person away, placing an unfair demand that can't be fulfilled.

EXERCISE

BE WITH YOUR LONGING

Explore your longing, allow yourself to fully feel it, and be with it. Sit and breathe into it. Your mind might want to know where this longing is coming from. See if you can allow yourself to be with it, even if you don't know why it is there. Let the fact that it is there be enough. Use the longing as a guide to opening your heart. Let the longing open you and breathe.

Lesson for Day Three

Ancestors

Yesterday, you learned about your connection to people who weren't born when you were and the longing that followed from having a "missing" sibling. Today we will look more closely at the lives and the love of the people that came before you.

Ancestors hold wisdom that they are very happy to share if we are open to hearing their messages. Just think about how many lives there were before you. Amongst all of them, many had tragic lives, weren't strong, and didn't learn much on planet earth, but because there are so many, you can be guaranteed that there is at least one soul who knew how to love and be healthy. The more you can honor the lives that have come before you, the more you can live and enjoy your own.

The mere act of giving life to another human being is the greatest gift one soul can give to another. Whether the parents raised that soul with love and abundance or whether they couldn't, on a soul level it doesn't matter very much. If you want to become whole, the realization that many people gave a lot in order for you to be born is very supporting.

Of course, I can blame World War II and what happened to my grandfather's parents and to my grandfather for me "suffering" and "wasting" the better part of my early life, but does that make me happy today and does it bring peace?

One of the first Constellations I participated in revealed the pain that my grandfather was carrying in his soul, but it also revealed the strength and courage my great-grandmother and great-grandfather had. It made it possible for me to put a face to the story and see that they are at peace. I went home after that Constellation and lit a candle for each of them, realizing that what I had thought to be the cause of my brokenness and my family's dysfunction wasn't at all so.

They were loving people who had been able to deal with their own fate. This realization was freeing me from feeling like I had to keep carrying the burden for them. In the Constellation, they literally asked me to give them back their pain and to not feel responsible for it. I gave back to them all the heaviness I had been carrying, as represented by a big stack of books. Again, when we are children, we unconsciously take on burdens that don't belong to us in an attempt to make our parents, grandparents or other close relatives happy. This is called *blind love* in Constellation terms. We let abuse happen out of this blind love.

I was subconsciousely telling my grandfather: "you can do anything with me if it only make you happy."

YOUR FEMALE LINEAGE

Each of us belongs to a male and female lineage, or line of ancestors. To visualize your female lineage, close your eyes and think of having your mother right behind you, her mother right behind her, her mother right behind her and so on. The same is true for your male lineage. Imagine your father right behind you, his father right behind him, and so on. I have seen and experienced through the Constellation work that most of us don't have our male or female lineage solidly lined up behind us. Again, the relationships between mothers and daughters, fathers and daughters, mothers and sons, and sons and fathers are mostly disrupted and disconnected. This disruption creates a great deal of pain for all souls involved.

On the contrary, a woman who has her lineages solidly "at her back" is strong and powerful.

Not having your male lineage behind you leaves you without guidance, wandering aimlessly through life. Not having your female lineage behind you makes you unable to receive and nurture yourself, and thus sustain a healthy life.

How does this disconnection between the generations happen?

From what I've been able to observe in many Constellations, it is almost impossible for a human being to give what she hasn't already received. If a woman, for example, lost her mother at a very young age and didn't receive motherly nurturing, then she in turn will have a hard time giving to her own daughter what she lacked herself. This again doesn't happen on a conscious level. The woman who lost her mother might very well be aware of how much she missed her mother and do everything to make sure that her daughter gets from her what she was missing. What then happens is that the mother doesn't really see the needs of her daughter but rather acts out of what she herself once needed.

This most likely results in the daughter not feeling seen by her own mother and growing up with a feeling of being disconnected. Only if you are able to meet your own needs are you able to understand and accept that others have their very own needs, too. You are also then able to realize that each person is a unique being with different needs, but all of them are valid.

One last point I want to share on female and male lineage before we move on is, that you not only are given life by the men and women who came before you, but you also inherit the strong beliefs that each lineage carries.

My client, Linda, struggled in love relationships her whole life. She even stopped being with men, because she just didn't feel safe. The work that we did together revealed that the women in her family held and passed on the belief that love puts you in danger when you are a woman, and that you will suffer and not survive if you listen to your feelings. Most likely for her great-great grandmother, or even farther back in the lineage, that was true. But for Linda in her own life, it really wasn't. Realizing that she was carrying a belief that belonged to her ancestor, she could let her fears about men go.

EXERCISE

RECONNECT WITH YOUR ANCESTORS

Today you are invited to reconnect with your ancestors. With all the good and all the bad. The good being the strengths and wisdom that all of them have and the bad being the limiting beliefs that got passed on. Pay attention to what beliefs and feelings are starting to pop up during your consciously connected breathing sessions. See if you can pinpoint beliefs that feel like they have been passed on to you and are not your own. When you encounter such a belief, find the feeling that lies underneath, stay with the feeling and breathe through it. Again, once you have awareness of it, a subconscious belief is lifted into your consciousness, and once it is conscious, it is no longer running your life.

For a recording of a guided ancestor meditation go to www. BlossomBook.com/recordings. This meditation will take 10 minutes. You can do it as often and at any time you'd like.

LESSON for Day Four

ORDERS OF LOVE

The theme of this week is stretching beyond your limits. For so many women I've worked with, learning about Family Constellations inspired them to expand and go deeper than they'd ever gone before. Looking at their family and their own situation has given my clients plenty of emotional material to work with, meaning deep-seated imprints that they are able to now access. As you do the same and old imprints surface in your life, remember to *sit and breathe*.

Let's look at the *orders of love* now, which is the spine of Family Constellations work.

The family system, just like any other system, has its own natural order. When that order is disrupted, the effects are felt by subsequent generations as the system tries to right itself. There appear to be certain natural laws operating to maintain that order and permit the free flow of love between family members. Hellinger described seven of these, calling them the "orders of love."

As you've already learned, a family system can be compared to a hanging mobile with many pieces dependent on each other for balance. When the love is flowing within a system and the orders of love are respected or in place, then there is peace and health within the system and the individual. When the orders of love are out of order, either systemic disease or disease in an individual soul manifests.

Today you'll be learning about the orders of love that Bert Hellinger first recognized and we're all able to see now in Family Constellation work. At first, these orders might seem strange to you, but when you tune into your soul and listen to them with the voice of your heart, you can hear a deeply resounding *yes, this is true!*

The first order states that all members of a family, an organism, or a system have an equal right to belong. When someone gets excluded from the family, organism, or system, because that person has done something wrong, had a different sexual orientation, or died and caused too much pain for the survivors— or for any other reason, it puts the family, organism or system as a whole out of balance.

Let's stay with the image of a mobile. Any imbalance causes the mobile to tip to one side. It's as if one part of the mobile got clipped off, and the whole mobile loses its balance and tips in the opposite direction.

The exclusion of one or several family members often doesn't happen consciously. My client, Sharon, came to me with the issue that people in her family were not talking with one another. She hadn't been allowed to talk with her father on his death bed, her mother didn't talk to her for years, and now her own son had turned away from her and was no longer speaking to her.

Of course, there were superficial reasons why one wasn't talking to the other. Sharon's son was mad because she had done something he disapproved of, Sharon's mother was mad because Sharon had left her husband after years of emotional abuse, and so on. But in Constellation work, the stories don't matter. What was apparent to me right from the beginning was the fact that there was a thread of people not talking to each other, and why that was, I had no idea.

In the Constellation, we set up Sharon's family of origin. She chose a representative for her mom, her sister, her father, herself, and also for her son, since the disturbed relationship with him was what caused her the most pain. In our initial conversation, Sharon had mentioned that she would have had an older brother but he died, and that her sister knew more about it than she did. I asked her to place all the representatives in the room and then to sit down.

The whole scene started quickly to take a life of its own. Sharon's son was on the opposite end of the room watching the four others. The main attention grabber was her father. He seemed in great anguish and despair. His representative moved aimlessly around as if he was looking for something. The sister seemed very mad, and the representative of Sharon somewhat lost and alone.

After the movement went on for some time, I told everyone that I wanted to try something different. The searching motions of the father indicated to me that he was looking for something. It could have been anything, but the one thing I knew about was that he had lost his son. None of the representatives knew what or who I was going to bring in. I asked a person in the circle if he would be willing to represent "that which the father is looking for." The man agreed and I asked him to lay flat on his back, right in front of the father's feet.

As soon as he had taken his place, the father collapsed over him, at first not being able to find any words to say. I asked him to speak the sentence, "When the pain gets too great, we don't talk in our family." The representative looked at me nodding and confirming that was so, and then he made this truth statement to the entire family.

The resolution in this Constellation was allowing the brother/son who had died so young to take his place in the family to be seen by his siblings, and also the pain of father and mother to be seen by the rest of the family. Once Sharon's father was allowed to mourn his dead child and introduce him to the rest of the family, the entire scene calmed down; everyone gathered around the father and the dead son, and they held and hugged each other. The final sentence from grandfather to grandson, the grandson being Sharon's son, was, "You are allowed to do it differently," meaning that he is allowed to show his feelings and talk about them.

In Sharon's case, the death of the sibling was so painful that his soul was excluded, and everyone pretended that he had never been born. The second order of love can be observed in her Constellation, which is that *early death affects the whole system*. Whether it is a child that was aborted, miscarried, or died early, or a child had to experience losing someone close early on, losing a loved one is always a very traumatic event.

The death of a loved one is traumatic in and of itself, but what is equally detrimental is when we are not allowed to give the dead a place in our life. This leads to exclusion of this soul and another imbalance in the soul of the individual and the family. Often what happens when a relative who died in an earlier generation isn't remembered, a younger soul will step into his or her place. The young soul is loyal to the one who died, unconsciously wanting to bring balance back to the family mobile.

In life, this loyalty to a dead ancestor can manifest as a death wish. The young soul is exclaiming, *I am not forgetting you; I will come and follow you.* Oftentimes I have come across a teenager who all of a sudden, despite a good home and nurturing care during his or her early years, develops a depression seemingly for no reason out of the blue. In these cases it often turns out that someone else in the family died at the exact same age of the teenager. By acknowledging the soul that had to die so young, the now living teenager can take his or her place again as a young living soul and the death wish is no longer needed.

WHAT'S YOUR RIGHT PLACE?

The third order of love has to do with everyone having their right place within the family mobile. Earlier members come first; it's a spatial order, the one born first, takes first place. If you take a place that isn't yours, it can have a detrimental effect on your soul and the soul of the system. This order has nothing to do with power or being "better than." It is simply the order in which we appeared on the planet. Your mother was before you, and if you have a younger sibling, you were born before him or her.

It is often seen in Constellations that children take the place of their parents.

Children think they are responsible for their parents' happiness, which adds much too heavy a burden on the child. It also doesn't allow the child to really live his or her life. Love and life go from big to small. Life is given from the parent to the child. When a child unconsciously claims to be her parents' parent, she is unable to take in life, which can manifest as depression or a wish to die, because life is a huge struggle and nothing is flowing towards her.

The fourth order of love is that *children are loyal to their parents, no matter what*. This can often be observed in victims of abuse. Children don't question what's happening to them again out of a kind of blind love. A child's love doesn't question.

Another kind of loyalty can be observed in children adhering to what we call the family conscience. The family conscience could be regarded as a set of unwritten rules for how things are done in a family; they have nothing to do with what's legal or generally seen as right. For example, if you are born into a Gypsy family, stealing is what you do to survive. If you don't steal, you don't belong. Or if you are born into a family where all firstborns become doctors, and you are the first born, you become a doctor. Unless we become aware of it, the family conscience often prevents us from exceeding our parents or doing things differently.

The fifth order of love states that *children will take on the feelings of others*. Again, this is because they think it is an act of love to do so—they want to help and make it better for another soul.

GIVING AND RECEIVING

The sixth order of love has to do with balance between giving and receiving, especially between the generations. In the sixth order, the *giving always goes from older to younger and the receiving from younger to older*. When this order is out of balance, for example when a mother expects to receive from the child, the child will feel as if she is being suffocated and will have no other choice than to separate and stay away.

The final order of love is that *children need to take life as it was given*. I mentioned this earlier when I talked about being your own parent. Again, Constellation work has shown that as long as you think you are entitled to something better, not realizing that the life you have is the right life for you, you suffer. When you can affirm your parents, then you can bow to the mystery of life. When you can say yes to both parts that you came from, you can say yes to who you are. When you accept reality and fate, then you can be free from entanglement.

Exercise

The Orders of Love for You

Reflect on the orders of love from the Family Constellations work. Looking at your own situation, which orders can you see are in place in your life and which aren't? How do you feel when being with the ones that are in place? How do you feel with the ones that aren't? Let the feelings come and breathe through them. Write any insights you have in your journal.

LESSON
for Day Five

LANGUAGE OF TRUTH

I mentioned at the beginning of Week Five, that when I first started teaching the Blossom Journey, the women in my classes were very interested in hearing how Family Constellation work helps to deal with sexual abuse. Everything I've shared about Constellations in the last few days helped them shift from having a closed heart into more openness, but what you are about to learn today is the specifics of Family Constellations and sexual abuse.

Family Constellation work looks at abuse in a very different way than traditional therapy or our society. Traditionally, sexual abuse is viewed in a very black and white manner. There is the perpetrator and the victim. The perpetrator is the evil that needs to get locked away, and most people think that when that happens (or if they could only make that happen), the victim and the family could find peace, because justice was done. Family Constellations reveal something very different, which is that the soul of the family of the perpetrator and the victim, and the soul of the victim and the perpetrator become entangled because of the wrong deed. Subsequently, they carry that load. I have seen cases in which the children of a perpetrator had a very difficult time in life, because they wanted to make up for their parent's wrongful behavior that they didn't even consciously know about.

One way that Constellation work brings peace to this situation is by helping to disentangle the family of the perpetrator from that of the victim. This can only happen when the perpetrator is left to his own fate and can then own his deed and the consequences.

Another aspect that is looked at differently in Constellation work is the role of the victim. Family Constellation has revealed that in most cases, when a daughter is sexually abused by her father, grandfather, uncle or mother's partner, it has to do with the women in her family not living their sexuality or using their sexuality in a manipulating way. When the mother looked to "punish" her husband by not having sex with him because he wasn't giving x-y-z to her, or because she herself was sexually traumatized, the daughter steps in for her.

My second Constellation involved my mother, her boyfriend, and me. The facilitator asked me to say to my mother, "I did it out of love for you." At first I couldn't utter the words, because my mind couldn't even comprehend what I'd been asked to say. The facilitator stated again, "Please, say to your mother, I did it out of love for you."

At the time, my relationship with my mother had come to an all time high in terms of tension. I had refused to come to my sister's confirmation ceremony as long as her boyfriend would share the same table. My whole family was outraged by my request that he not be invited. Things had really escalated, which was odd for my family, since both my parents were into personal growth and spiritual development, but when old stuff comes up, it comes up mightily. No one wants to deal with sexual abuse in the family, yet it's going on in almost every family I know. The one who suffered the most was my dear little sister, because I ended up not coming to her big day.

Needless to say, my heart was in great pain, thus the Constellation.

And now I was being asked to say, "I did it out of love for you, Mama." Eventually I said it, and strangely enough it felt right on a core level. Even though the experience was "just" a Constellation, for the first time I felt seen and acknowledged.

The healing sentence between mother and daughter, "I did it out of love for you," meaning the daughter allowed the abuse to happen out of love for her mother, often brings great relief to both mother and daughter.

When I introduce this concept, some women feel outraged. They think that this statement means that the abuse is their fault. The abuse was absolutely wrong and the perpetrator is 100 percent responsible for it. Nevertheless, the truth also is that the child often didn't question what was happening, out of love.

Every time I have participated in or facilitated a Constellation around sexual abuse, this sentence, or a variation of it, has brought great relief.

Before we go on to the exercise of the day, I wanted to share a little bit more with you about what the healing sentences are. As you have learned through the Constellations examples given so far, Constellation facilitators will suggest sentences for the representatives to say to each other. It is a language of essence or truth that is free of blame and reactivity, a language based on the truth of the soul. This language in Constellation terms is called the "language of the soul."

If we were to use our everyday language in Constellations, we wouldn't get very far because we would only be able to deal

with things on the level of the ego—and not the egos of the people that are represented but most likely the egos of the people doing the representing. At first, this language of the soul seems to be very odd. But after observing its effects, you can see that it brings about wholeness.

The healing sentences stay with the facts. For example, there might be a child who has been very badly treated by her parents, and instead of telling the parents how angry she is with them, and trying to make them apologize or needing them to apologize, it brings much more peace to her soul if she can simply say to her mother, "You are my mother, you carried me in your womb for nine months, you gave me life."

Those are the facts.

Another example of a healing sentence would be for a child to say to his or her parents "I am the little one, you are the big one." This is a hard one to say for many of us, because, again, we have decided that our parents don't know what they are doing, and that we have to become the parents because we know better. This gives us a feeling of superiority but also adds a great burden to our life. It is not the order of love or life. The order of love says that parents are the big ones, children are the little ones, the children take from their parents, and parents give to their children.

Again, that parents are the bigger ones is not a value judgment. It doesn't say they are better because they are bigger, nor does it say they can do whatever they want with you because you are smaller. To be the little one doesn't mean you are devoid of rights. It is simply a statement of order, something very natural. If we were working with the ego here, we would be stuck,

because the ego attaches so much value, judgment and feelings to the idea of being the little one or being the big one. The soul simply recognizes that this is a truth and can relax.

The language of the soul also doesn't ask for forgiveness. Asking you to forgive me if I harmed you puts the burden onto you. It is much more powerful for both of us if I can own up and say that I am sorry and that I have wronged you. Again, this is especially freeing to hear from the "person" who sexually abused you. Asking you to forgive the person who inflicted all the pain on you is asking you to do something to make him feel better.

If your perpetrator can look you in the eye and say, "I am sorry, for I have wronged you," it takes the burden off your shoulders and puts it back on his.

I always invite my clients to use the language of the soul in their daily lives. Whenever they do, they tell me that it has created a lot of closeness and peace in their intimate relationships.

EXERCISE

USING THE LANGUAGE OF THE SOUL

Today I invite you to be with the sentence: *I did it out of love.* Journal about your answers to the questions: *What does that sentence mean to you? What does it bring up for you?* If it activates your nervous system, if it triggers you, sit and breathe through the sensations.

BONUS

Start using the language of truth. For example, when you do something "wrong," say to the other person simply, *I'm sorry I've wronged you.* In this way, you emphasize your full responsibility for what you have done. Or, if you feel like your child is taking on the role of parenting you by telling you when you can do something or not, tell your child calmly and in a matter of fact tone, *I am the big one and you're the little one. I'm making this decision.* Again, you are taking responsibility without blaming the other. Often parents are afraid to do this, and instead look to the child for approval and decision making. By using the words in the above sentences, you bring healing, balance and a sense of rightness to your relationships.

LESSON for Day Six

INSIGHTS

Today I want to share a few more insights gained from the Constellation work that helped the women in my groups at this point on their journey before we move on to the next steps. The reading will be short today, because you'll get to do a fun project.

The first insight I wanted to share today is, that the truth never hurts.

With our everyday logical mind, we think that if we are honest with someone, we might hurt their feelings. Here is a trivial example. You are sitting across from your friend and the zipper of her pants is open, but you don't want to tell her, because she might feel embarrassed.

Here is a not-so trivial example. My client Brenda's father left her and her mother when Brenda was two. Rather than telling Brenda who her father was, her mother decided to tell her that he had died. Her mother did this because in her mind it gave Brenda the illusion that she was loved by her father and that he was a good man. Her mother also thought it would stop Brenda from looking for her father and finding out that he didn't love her enough to stay. Her mother truly thought she was protecting Brenda from future pain.

Fortunately or unfortunately, lies don't hold up in a Constellation and also not on a soul level. The truth is ultimately what heals and sets us free. It was painful for Brenda to hear her father's representative in the Constellation say, "I didn't love you enough to stay," but it had a very freeing effect on her, because it was the truth. Brenda was able to connect on a different, more real level with her father. And because of that, with all men.

The next insight I want to share is that we all have our own fate.

Having worked as a psychotherapist for over 15 years, I have come across many overwhelming fates that people have. But it is even more striking to see in every single Constellation, if a person is denied carrying out their fate, (for example, if a child takes on the pain of the father or mother in an attempt to ease their pain), it is harder for the person with the "tragic fate," and causes disharmony and imbalance in the entire system. I have seen it time and time again how when a perpetrator accepts his fate, the whole system can land in peace. It's as if the soul of a perpetrator is trapped in "nowhere land" and his whole clan suffers until the truth comes to light. Even if that means admitting that you murdered, raped or abused someone. And not just admitting, but *owning* that deed.

The last insight I want to share with you is that everyone always does the best he or she can, given the circumstances. Every human being is inherently good. Some people just have more resources or better circumstances than others in life. But everyone always does the best they can under any given circumstance. This is a hard concept to swallow and again isn't meant to negate the wrongness of bad deeds. But in working with many clients, I've observed how holding a belief about the people that harmed you, seeing them as worthless because they are inherently bad, doesn't help your growth.

Exercise

Family Abode

In the beginning, I mentioned that today you'd get to do a fun activity. This activity will bring everything you have learned this week together. You are going to make a "family abode." A family abode is like an altar. It's an art history project. *Your* art and *your* family history. You can build your abode in 3D on a tray or flat on a poster board. See if you can find pictures of the people you are entangled with and the ones that give you strength. Also add one or two items that connect you to your strength, like a picture of your animal totem or your favorite color. This altar will give you something to look at that lets you consciously align with your wholeness.

At times, my abode or altar had pictures of me when I was three (my "broken" time), and my mother and grandmother. A golden color, because for me the golden sun is the most healing. A rose, because for me a rose is a perfect representation of beauty, love, and wholeness.

Make it a practice to sit for a few minutes in the morning and evening in front of your family abode, and let it speak to you.

And again, don't forget to breathe.

Lesson for Day Seven

WEEK FIVE IN REVIEW

In Week Five you learned that in order for you to integrate your trauma, your core wounds, it is important to see all that has come before you and to realize you are part of something bigger, that you are the sum total of it all.

You can use the technique of Consciously Connected Breathing to integrate your stuff by simply being with your emotions when your nervous system is activated and you are triggered. If you encounter a pattern that just won't go away, or if you are in crisis, Family Constellation work is recommended. (See Recommended Resources page.)

You learned that:

> *There are certain orders of love, and when they are not present, the whole system/family suffers.*
>
> *We get entangled with people we love and take on their fate.*
>
> *Language of the soul helps the love to start flowing.*
>
> *Both truths hold: people do their best and what they do is wrong at times.*

The more you realize how interconnected you are, the more that realization will allow you to live your own life. As long as you deny where you come from or try to live a falsely independent life, you will struggle in life. When you are able to be grateful and to live a life that honors all that you are, you will be connected to your true power.

As the final two weeks of your Blossom Journey approach, it's time to arrive in your body, in the present moment, so that in the final step of the journey you can meet yourself, your lover, and the world in trust, power, and intimacy.

EXERCISE

REFLECT BACK

Reflect back at Week Five of your Blossom Journey. Take out your journal and write your answers to these questions: *What was most helpful to you in this week's lessons? What kinds of shifts can you already see within yourself and in the beliefs you have been holding? What is starting to change in your life?*

Write what comes to you.

Week Six
OWN ALL OF WHO YOU ARE

Before you can fully meet the world in wholeness and follow your bliss, which is the "goal" for the Blossom Journey and the theme for the next and the final week, it is necessary that you learn to own yourself. This means you reclaim all the parts and dreams you left behind and step into your true power. You live the life you want to live and not the life you are fated to live because of the programming you came into the world with and received growing up.

This is what Week Six of the Blossom Journey is about. Owning yourself also means that in any given moment (or at least in most moments), you have the ability to make a choice about your reaction and behavior. It means that you have attained a certain amount of awareness and freedom in this life and you have integrated a good portion of your trauma so that you know what to do when you are triggered and activated. It also means that you have the skills and experience to break the chain of trauma and drama, and you are able to have peaceful relationships. You no longer feel that others have power over you, that you have to sacrifice yourself for the greater good, but rather you allow yourself to have needs and to feel pleasure, that you allow yourself to just *be* and enjoy your life.

When you own yourself, you no longer feel that you need permission from another to live and create the life you want. Owning yourself enables you to stay open-hearted in a relationship with another and the world, even when you feel hurt. You might still slam the door when you get angry, but it will not lead to an immediate divorce.

The reason why you react to certain things more than to others is that your primary wounds are engraved into your physiology. Trauma gets literally imprinted into your body's make up. It impacts your nervous system. When trauma has happened, you end up wired differently. Trauma does not just get engraved into your own nervous system but also into the bodies of the people who came before you.

We can speculate about karma and the intangible stuff we inherit from our ancestors, but it is a scientific fact that you do inherit the physiological make up, and, if there has been trauma, the effects of trauma from previous generations. It's like the programming that comes with the computer if your body were a computer. (The science that does research in this field is called *epigenetics*. Its findings are fascinating and worth exploring.)

This week, we will take a look at what happens in your body when trauma occurs. This will explain why simply being with your emotions and feeling them is such a powerful practice. It will also give you a further explanation as to why Family Constellations work so well. Furthermore, it will give you yet another tool and awareness that will help you lift yourself out of the dark and into the light.

This week you are taking what is "living knowledge" in you and making sense of it. You could have learned everything that you are learning this week at the beginning of this journey, but it would probably not have made much sense. It's not about mental understanding—it's about *living knowledge*. Everything you will be learning this week will make sense to you because you have journeyed through it in the past five weeks.

LESSON
for Day One

THE PHYSIOLOGY OF TRAUMA

Today, let's look at the body's make up and the changes that occur when trauma happens.

Your physical body gives you the ability to experience life, it gives you the greatest joy, and it can give you the greatest pain. Without it, you would not be living this life.

Most of my clients perceive their bodies, especially as females, as a source for a lot of pain, both physical and emotional. I ask them if they can remember how they felt when they were little, how much pleasure they got from running, splashing water, being held, petting a dog. I ask them if they can see that without their body, there would be no "them" and no pleasure, no joy in this lifetime. They often nod in agreement and then start to cry. They tell me how sad they are to have lost the ability to experience simple pleasure throughout their bodies.

Your body holds the key to heaven or hell. It is up to you to have this realization and to act upon it. The only thing that will ever be real is the present moment, the joy and the pleasure that you experience in and through your body, it's paradise. When you are trapped in the past or the future, it almost always equals hell. A lot of the work on this journey is aimed at getting you into your body, because your body is always in the present moment. When you are in the present moment, you are free. Free of mental prison.

For most of my clients, physical activity brings them back into their bodies when their head is too spun out. Dancing, sports, breathing, yoga, love-making… All these physical activities can bring you back into your body. You have to work with your body if you ever want to become whole.

Let's look at why, when trauma happens, it becomes so hard to stay in your body. To understand what happens on a physiological level, you first have to look at your brain and nervous system.

Your brain consists of three parts (I am giving you a very simplified version). The *reptilian* brain, the *mid-brain* and the *neocortex*.

The reptilian brain, as its name suggests, is the oldest part of your brain, in charge of all of the instinctual responses of the nervous system. It also rules over all the autonomic processes that are going on in your body, such as digestion, breathing, and heartbeat. The reptilian brain is the home to the fight-or-flight reflex and instinctual trauma response.

The midbrain is the smallest region of the brain that acts as a sort of relay station for auditory and visual information. The midbrain controls many important functions, such as your visual and auditory systems, as well as eye movement. Portions of the midbrain are involved in the control of body movement.

The neocortex is what distinguishes you as a human from animals and enables you to make decisions, have a conscience, and know what is right or wrong. You are only able to access the higher parts of your brain when the reptilian brain does not sense danger. (I say "higher parts," because the midbrain and the neocortex literally sit on top of the reptilian brain in the structure of your brain.)

When you look at where the brain connects to the spinal column, you see the spinal cord which brings together the nerves that run through your body. Most signals from your body travel along the spinal cord in and out of the brain. The spinal cord and the brain make up the *central nervous systems*, that part of your nervous system that "decides".

The spinal cord enters and exits from the reptilian brain. This makes the reptilian brain the first "decision-making department." From there, the information gets processed and the reptilian brain decides on further action. Either it sends the signals right out the spinal cord and into the branches of the *peripheral nervous system*, into the nerves of your body, or it passes further decision-making on to the mid and higher brain.

The reptilian brain only decides to pass information on to the mid and higher brain if it is in a calm state. This means you only have access to your higher brain when your reptilian brain is not in fight-or-flight. When you are in reaction, your fight-or-flight response is activated, and you do not have access to your more "human" or higher brain (as opposed to reptilian). Because your nervous system has experienced trauma, it is rarely in a calm state and more often in fight-or-flight. This means that you mostly make instinctual decisions and not necessarily the best or wisest ones. You basically make decisions while you are "running away" or fleeing from an assumed dangerous situation. The problem is that you often run away from situations that are not dangerous.

It's not just you. Most of us in today's fast paced society have nervous systems that are continually triggered and overwhelmed in fight or flight mode.

Because you wrongly assess the situation as being dangerous when it is not, you make wrong decisions (like, you start to fight or hide). Unless the trauma in the nervous system is resolved, you are unable to "see" that you are running away from old ghosts, not anything real. You are unable to react appropriately to most situations. This in essence creates a lot of drama.

The trauma imprints in your nervous system are the emotional memories that you learned about earlier in the context of core wounds, emotional imprints, and the trash in the trash can.

You unconsciously use these imprints as filters through which you perceive life. This essentially is a very clever survival strategy, but only that. It only helps you to survive and nothing more. It keeps you at survival level. Fun and pleasure are not necessary to survive. You stay at a survival level, because instead of really seeing what is happening in the moment, you assume what is happening based on your past experiences and you react. You constantly see and create your life through the filter of your past.

You become like the bull in the bullring that expects that something upsetting is going to happen whenever a red cloth appears. Red cloth always equals upset, and therefore the bull can't do any differently than get defensive and race forward in fear. He has an emotional imprint that triggers him getting mad when he sees a red cloth flashing before his eyes. Now, when you encounter something that looks like what you have encountered before, and it wasn't good for you, you react in defense. This *something*, whether it is really dangerous for you or not, acts as trigger.

When you are triggered, you only have access to the memory of the past. The memory of the past is what you are reacting to and not the actual situation that is in front of you. As long as you are seeing this moment through the filter of your past, as long as you are seing the red blanket as something that is upsetting, you are not free. You even recreate the past, in a way, and end up feeling like you are stuck in the same old rut.

The number one complaint that I hear from my clients is that they end up in the same situation, no matter how hard they try to change. I teach them what I shared in the previous paragraph.

Most of the insights gained in this section come from working with the findings and research results of Peter A. Levine, an American therapist, author and educator who specializes in the treatment and understanding of chronic stress, more commonly known as *post-traumatic stress disorder*. Levine has dedicated his life to the task of understanding what happens physiologically during trauma and finding ways to reverse the impact that trauma has on the nervous system.

In his work, he stayed close to nature and observed how animals deal with trauma. He also used the phenomenological approach like Bert Hellinger. The reason why he assumed early on in his work that he would find answers to his questions about trauma healing in the animal world is simple. Even though we are farther developed than animals, we still share a great deal of our neurological make up with them.

As previously mentioned, like all other mammals and even reptiles, you have a reptilian brain, the instinctual part of your brain. This part responds when you are in danger. Again, this part of the brain is home to the fight-or flight-mechanism, which means that when you are in danger, you respond partly as animals do. The main actors in the fight or flight response are the *sympathetic* and the *parasympathetic nervous systems*. Both of these big branches of nerves regulate your body's functions by controlling the hormone cocktail in your blood and by regulating many other very intricate and complicated biochemical processes.

In regard to trauma, animals often fare much better than humans do. Animals rely solely on their instinctual response to threats. A fast running jaguar will run, a hedgehog will curl up into a tight ball. As human beings, we have developed more strategies for survival over time. The caveman had very few options available when faced with an overwhelming threat. We also developed the limbic/emotional brain and the neocortex, our rational brain. Now, when faced with a threat, one of our higher developed brain parts might get in the way of our instinctual response. Instead of fighting for our survival, we are confused and unable to react. We freeze. Or we energetically leave our bodies. This freezing is like burning the trauma almost irrevocably into our nervous system.

Levine gives the example of 30 kidnapped children who were held captive in a trailer buried underground. Of the 30 children, 29 froze in fear. Only one of them started looking for a way out and eventually freed the others. Of the 30 children, 29 showed long-term physiological and psychological post-traumatic stress syndromes; the one who was able to act and move didn't show any.

The way we respond to trauma is only one part of the equation. The second part of this equation is how we recover from it. And it's not by talking about it.

If an animal survives a threat by means of their survival response, they are able to discharge the enormous amounts of energy generated during the threat and their individual response, in their nervous system and body. They will shake, tremble, make sounds and move until the activation is discharged; this is a natural, instinctual process initiated and carried out by the reptilian brain. The animal does not show any signs of psychological or physiological damage after this discharge has occurred. It will go on with its life as if nothing had ever happened.

As human beings, we generally do not have the space or the instinct to let our nervous system discharge after a threat or traumatic event. Our nervous system will stay in its frozen state. Or at least parts of it will. Levine suggests that the long-term post traumatic symptoms are not caused by the triggering event itself but by the frozen energy that we haven't been able to discharge. This frozen energy can wreak havoc on our bodies, minds and spirits.

Trauma in our culture is often defined in terms of the event that caused it. This can make it difficult for the healing process, since certain events are bound to be more impactful than others. I have learned to look at trauma through a different lens, the lens of the individual's symptoms. What may impact one human being severely might not even faze another. Factors like age, general health, temperament and many others play a role in determining the severity of one's presenting symptoms. Should we treat all people by the same standard? I don't think so, but unfortunately that is often what happens in our medical system.

In my work, I don't look so much at the event but at the person who is in front of me and at the symptoms he or she is describing to determine to what degree the trauma is affecting his or her nervous system.

Symptoms of Trauma

Symptoms of trauma can be very far reaching, but they all have one thing in common, which is they render "the victim" helpless. Whether the symptoms are of a psychological or physical nature doesn't matter. For us to truly become whole again, we need to understand the physiological aspects of trauma as well as those that are psychological. In order for us to truly blossom, we need to take the integration out of the mere psychological realm and look at integration from a holistic standpoint.

Levine's findings gave answers to my questions of why Constellations work, why shamanistic healing works, and why Consciously Connected Breathing works. I love when science (in this case, neuroscience) explains the ancient wisdom or spiritual approaches. When you are sitting with your breath or when you are watching a Constellation, those are moments in which some of the frozen energy in your nervous system can be released. You can literally feel how heat leaves your body, how your nervous system releases, and how you become calmer, more flexible, and more fluid.

EXERCISE

JUST BE

Today the exercise is to just be with what you learned today.

Lesson
for Day Two

The Connection Between
the Physical and the Spiritual

To understand today's lesson, which is deepening your under-standing of your body so that you can learn how to fully come back into it, let me share with you what I have come to believe is our entire makeup.

Most of us have no problem acknowledging that we are physi-cal beings. And also most of us (at least the ones living in Cal-ifornia, Austin, or Concorde) have no problem acknowledging that we are spiritual beings having a physical experience. But what does all of this mean in reality? How can we make use of the knowledge that we are spiritual beings, and not just use it as a bandage when life doesn't feel good on earth? How can we make use of the knowledge that we are spiritual beings for more than using it as justification for our non-participation in life by telling ourselves, "It's okay, I am just a spiritual being having a rather unwanted human experience, which will soon be over, so I'll just stick it out until I can go back and be a happy angel again ..."

Here is the answer: thinking you are a spiritual being that is separate from your body is a fallacy. Your body is your spirit. We are often taught that the body is a vehicle and that the spirit is only using it, that you are a spiritual being using your body to experience life, but your troubles come from seeing your body and your spirit as separate. Your body is your spirit manifest in the material plane. The two are inseparable.

Here is what my experience has taught me. We all are a composite of four "bodies." We have a physical body, an emotional body, the mental body, and a fourth one, the one that most people don't talk about, the *vibrational* body. The vibrational body is that part of you which is closest to God (the universe or whatever you call that power). If you were to look at all four of these bodies in terms of frequencies, speeds, density and colors, you would perceive the physical body as the darkest colored, most dense, slowest moving, lowest vibrating one—that's why you can see and feel it. Next in line would be the mental body. The mental body is very much connected to your physical body and living in time—the past and future. The mental body is the one that dictates most of your life because you believe what it tells you.

The emotional body is the bridge between the physical plane and the spiritual, or vibrational, plane. The emotional body vibrates at a higher frequency than the mental body, but not quite as high as the vibrational body. What we all want, even though we are not speaking about it in these terms yet, is to be up to speed with our vibrational body so we can be free and be who we truly are. A lot of traditions tell us to get rid of earthly desires, emotions, and our ego to achieve enlightenment, but the truth is you can only experience enlightenment as a human incarnated on earth in a body.

You cannot be fully human if you lose any one of your four bodies. You also cannot be enlightened if you lose one of your four bodies, or if you don't fully own and use them.

So the real path to enlightenment, in my opinion, is through elevation of our three lower vibrating bodies to the higher frequency of our vibrational body. In other words, when you tune yourself to the frequency of your highest self vibrationally, you are nearing enlightenment. The instrument you have been given to do this is your life.

The pursuit of pleasure can be your compass, and your ability to allow yourself pure pleasure and joy is a great indicator that you are moving in the right direction.

Through your body you can release and become free to move forward without reliving your story everyday and without having it define you. You can come to a place where *yes*, you were abused and *yes*, you suffered a great deal and experienced a long, dark night of the soul, but still you are able to be in love and have the fullest life now.

You are able to be in love with life, yourself and your lover. To *be love*. To feel joy and pleasure. As a woman, if you are like me and most of my clients, you are most happy and fullfilled when you can be love, pure joy, and fully able to experience pleasure. When you can live with an open heart, when you don't have to protect yourself, guard yourself, "be your own man," and close down in hurt.

When we are young children, we are living mainly in our vibrational body. Or better said, the vibrational body is the only one that is fully developed. Our physical, mental and emotional bodies still need a lot of development before they can be a container for the vibrational body.

Sexual energy is a very strong force and vibration—it is raw, it creates, and it destroys. When the body of a young child encounters sexual energy, it doesn't have the capacity to contain the experience, and it literally blows its fuses. This is a very painful experience. Consciously your world collapses, physically you might have to endure great pain, emotionally it's unbearable, and energetically it catapults you right out of your body.

You see, all your four bodies are interwoven and your nervous system is the physical translator of the vibrational. Through the Blossom Journey your nervous system has already become your trusted friend. When you are triggered, your nervous system is in activation, and when you are centered your nervous system is in balance. Peace is an experience of a balanced nervous system in a human body. A nervous system is only balanced when body, mind, and spirit are in sync.

Levine developed a psychotherapy approach that is called *Somatic Experiencing* which suggests that by just being present to the sensations in your body, you integrate them. His work basically confirmed what I had learned and experienced through my own work with Family Constellations and the Presence Process.

Levine agrees that there is no need to know the story. Many of my clients know that early abuse happened but the memories are very faint and unclear, so this is very comforting to know. You do not need to remember every detail nor relive it. If you have symptoms, meaning your nervous system goes into fight-or-flight a lot, that is proof that you experienced trauma.

As you now know, it takes some practice to do the integration work, because your mind wants to understand what is happening, it wants to make sense of everything.

Generally, after someone has watched and experienced a Constellation, I invite them to simply contain the experience. By *containing* I mean to stay with it in their body by putting their feeling/sensing attention on it. A lot of my clients have the hardest time with this. They are so used to doing therapy or self-development courses and then implementing a new behavior or practicing a new affirmation or belief they have learned.

In my opinion, all of this is unnecessary and takes too much energy and mental focus. It also takes the freedom and fun out of life. The difference between learning a new behavior and practicing it, and simply integrating the trauma by sensing it, is that with the former you are merely reprogramming your brain using an old pathway. In the latter case, you create a new pathway that doesn't even know the old one existed.

EXERCISE

SLOW MOVEMENT

The best way to connect to your body and to synchronize all four bodies is through movement. Today I invite you to spend 15 minutes with the Slow Movement exercise that I have recorded for you at www.BlossomBook.com/recordings.

Slowing down your movement makes you come home into your body. The invitation is to feel your body from the inside out. Again this is an exercise which will strengthen your "feeling capacity" muscle. This exercise specifically helps you to own your body and to develop a sense of being safe, because you are "home."

Lesson for Day Three

SOUL RETRIEVAL

Tribal cultures, both ancient and current, have a different way of dealing with trauma than us civilized people. They know that trauma is part of life, and although they might not know the neurophysiology and biochemistry behind trauma, they do know that the soul leaves the body and must be reunited to make the victim whole. In some cultures, there are chosen people who have dedicated their lives to learning how to do that work, known as shamans, medicine men, and wise ones. We have come quite far in our Western medicine and science, but in the end this proves that ancient wisdom had it right all along.

In the past week, I have mentioned several times that we leave our bodies when we experience trauma. Today we are going to look at what happens and how we can bring the part that leaves back, the way a shaman would do. Again, I love being alive today because we are able to be our own shaman, to be enlightened and initiated, something that even 100 years ago was unthinkable.

Back to leaving the body, splitting your soul off from your body and leaving life. It's a great strategy for survival, but it is only that. Have you ever observed a small child playing from the time he or she wakes up until it's time to go to bed and still not tired but wanting to play more, having too much energy left to call it the end of the day?

Children are a pure life force if not forced out of their bodies. You were pure life force once. You want this life force, this un-bridled energy, back again. And the only way to get it back is to gradually create a safe place in your body for the parts that have left to re-enter and participate in life. Shamans know all about this. In their language this process is called *soul retrieval*. They travel to either the middle world, the lower world, or the upper world to find the lost soul and bring it back.

In this step of the Blossom Journey, I take my clients on a meditative journey. I have them close their eyes and imagine walking down a grassy path, much like the meditation you did to reconnect with your little one in Week Two. Then I have them go into a forest. I remember doing this with my client Norah. While she was journeying, she told me how she ended up deep in the forest in a cave, and in the farthest, darkest, womblike corner of that cave, her child-self, the missing part of her soul, was curled up and withdrawn from the world. I encouraged her to start a conversation to find out what her child needed to come out of this place and to follow her back into the real world because the child was a vital part of her and without her Norah couldn't fully live her life. It took some time for the little one to even lift her head and look at her. Norah reported back that she had nothing but love for this child, and the child felt this. I suggested she ask the child if a helper was needed, like an animal or spirit guide. A golden retriever dog appeared. The little child jumped on and rode on the dog while holding Norah's hand all the way back home through the imaginary forest and into my office.

After this imaginative experience, Norah felt warm and more complete in her chest. Feelings of warmth almost always accompany the integration of an emotional imprint and the opening of the heart.

Exercise

Goal Retrieval Through Art

1. Get your art supplies out. You will be painting or drawing, so you need paper and crayons. Next close your eyes and ask that part of you that split off to go into another "world" to show herself. When you start getting a sense of her, start drawing. Once you feel your drawing is complete, spend time with it. See if she is willing to come back into your world of today. Find out if she needs something specific from you that will enable her to come back. Keep the picture with you until you feel she is integrated. This might take a few hours, some days, or a week.

When you feel that this process is complete, release the picture by burning it. Thank her for not completely disappearing, for waiting for you to come get her and deciding to come back and be a part of you.

2. After you have re-established a connection with this part of yourself, recall together with her what her dream was when she was little. Allow this dream to become your fuel for transformation and the future creation of your life. Write your dream down and read it often.

LESSON for Day Four

BOUNDARIES

The theme for Week Six, as you know, is owning yourself fully. Knowing how to feel your own boundaries and knowing how to lovingly communicate those boundaries to others plays a big part in owning yourself. Your boundaries and your awareness of them are both very much connected to your body.

When you leave your body because of trauma, you also leave behind the ability to feel your boundaries clearly and so lose the ability to protect yourself. Often it seems that victims of trauma attract harmful events to them like magnets. This happens partly because, as mentioned, a traumatized person has left their body.

Most of the clients I see are very sensitive beings. They not only left their bodies partly after the trauma, but they also developed a radar-like sensing organ that can tell them when danger is miles away, or so they think. What this radar-like organ does is pull them out of their bodies even more, and it makes it more difficult for them to stay within themselves and feel anything. They need to retrain their body to stop constantly sensing what's going on around them. They need to learn not to care what others do, think or vibe, and stop reacting in a way that reflects what they think another wants.

There was a time in my life when I was working as a barista in a very nice little Italian café. I was tormented by feeling like I knew every thought that was going on in the minds of the people around me. I was so worried about how they perceived me, that all my attention was on them. It was exhausting. All I wanted was to feel at peace with who I was.

It turned out that I was way "out there." I had just had an eye-opening session with a teacher from India who spoke to me about boundaries and how women who have been sexually abused learn to always be "out there" energetically and not feel their boundaries. I could absolutely understand what he'd been telling me as I was observing myself during my work at the café. He had shared with me that while "being out there" was a good skill for survival, it never allowed anyone to truly, emotionally come close, because it literally creates an energetic push away feeling to the other person as if invisible tentacles are patting him or her down. Also, it doesn't allow us to be truly seen, creating an energetic field that acts like an invisible deflecting screen all around us. The deflecting screen looks to the others' subconscious like sparkles radiating outward. And as you probably know sparkles are a nice package to invite all kinds of unwanted attention.

My Indian teacher had also told me that only people who are insensitive or emotionally unavailable unconsciously sense the invisible patting down and those will be the ones coming on to us, because they take it as an invitation. He explained how that worked: sexually abused women have an energetic hole where their sexual center is; so right in our belly below the navel, there is emptiness. I felt he was right, because I could sense nothing there. He stated that the woman might not feel very sexual, but when she interacts with men, that energetic hole is perceived by them like a kaleidoscope. It draws them in and bedazzles them.

As a woman, it can feel very powerful to have that ability to be-dazzle, but when it happens unconsciously, we are putting our-selves in danger, because we are signaling that we want to have sex without even knowing we are doing that. We do not feel our own boundaries, and we do not own ourselves and our energy.

A small percentage of women sense that this is going on sub-consciously and have turned off their female sexuality com-pletely. If you are one of them, still read the next part.

Let's look now at how you can close this energetic hole and start owning your sexuality and becoming fully aware of your boundaries.

At first, you'll have to wean yourself off your sparkly super powers, at least with people you don't really want to engage with sexually. You do that by becoming aware of where your energy is when you are interacting with others. Is it on the oth-er? Are you trying to read the other and please the other (even if it is by being contrary or obnoxious)? When you feel like your energetic attention is on the other person, pull your en-ergetic attention back into your lower belly. Use your sensing and feeling capacity to do that. Start to care more about what is going on in you, not in him or her.

I want to give you a word of caution, because again, life might feel kind of boring for a while without having all the drama of attraction going on, but trust me, it is also getting more real.

When I first turned off my own sparkle powers, I thought men didn't like me anymore.

I had based a big portion of my self-worth on the responses I got from men, because of the energetic magic show I was al-ways radiating. (Don't get me wrong, there is nothing wrong or dangerous about a woman's radiance when she owns her power. Sparkle powers are just not an authentic radiance.) Every morning, when I walked into the cafe, I was used to at least three Italian waiters and the chef whistling *ciao bella*, getting a smack on my butt from a co-worker, then getting tipped really well all day long from the men coming to drink coffee at the café. When I changed, I couldn't keep working, giving out coffee and lots of my sparkles. But I met people who I started having real relationships with. I started having friends. Female friends. And that was new for me.

Energetically owning your sexuality and keeping your energy more consciously within yourself can help tremendously in becoming aware of your own boundaries. Then comes the challenge of communicating those boundaries, so that they will be respected and firmly in place.

Many of my clients have to learn this the hard way. They might know their limits, but they can't seem to get other people to see and respect them. It often takes them becoming completely exhausted before realizing that they are letting others dictate their needs.

Many of my clients who have children make the mistake of thinking that saying yes to everything is expressing unconditional love for their children. They trick themselves into thinking that when they say yes, their child is happy, and when their child is happy, they are happy. Not only do they set themselves up for complete failure because no one person can be the sole source of happiness of another, but they completely give themselves up. Part of their desperation is that they only know how to set boundaries through anger and punishment, and they don't want to do that. They don't want to scream and yell at their children, and if they do, they beat themselves up for days. They don't know how to communicate their boundaries in a loving way.

One of my teachers once said, *"No"* is a complete sentence. We never have to get angry at our children." The moment you get angry you have lost yourself and given your power away. Staying with yourself energetically helps to communicate your boundaries in a loving way.

Exercise

Turn on the Real You

Try turning off your sparkle power as you go about interacting with others during your day. Simply observe yourself when talking with men and women, particularly when you want something from someone. Sense in your body and see if you can find the hole I have been talking about.

Notice when you use your sparkle power to manipulate and attempt to control. Know that whenever you are doing that, you are moving away from intimacy, love and connection with another and into separation and loneliness. Energetically put your attention only on yourself and do not concern yourself about what is going on "over there."

LESSON for Day Five

SENSITIVITY IS AN ASSET

I've noticed that when some of my clients first learn about boundaries, as you did yesterday, they think they have to become tough in order to set boundaries, and they don't want to. Here is the thing. We can be gentle and sensitive yet still clear about what is acceptable and what is not.

I teach my clients to be self advocates by knowing their limits. To know what they can tolerate and what they can't helps them to create the space they need to be sensitive. It's a good thing to be sensitive.

Being sensitive manifests in many forms. For example, being a picky eater, something that is not welcome in our society. My client, Joan, learned to be polite and not take care of her own needs around food. When she dined out with family or friends, she always ate what everyone else was eating. The consequence was that she often experienced an upset stomach.

Today, Joan doesn't do that anymore because she understands that being a picky eater is another way of listening to herself and recognizing her boundary. Someone who is sensitive can listen without words needing to be said. And by listening, I mean truly seeing the other person and hearing their needs. It all starts with you.

Use this gift for yourself first.

Many of my clients have been ridiculed most of their lives for being too sensitive. They put on the disguise of the tough bride, the shy wallflower, or the funny clown, but underneath all that, you and I know it's not who they really are or who they long to be.

It took me 31 years to realize that there is nothing wrong with being sensitive. Because of having sensitive systems, we have to take care of our bodies and our psyches a little differently than another would. Nobody is ridiculed for putting on a sweater when it is cold. I was constantly made fun of for my picky way of eating. Boyfriends would roll their eyes and call me "high maintenance." What they didn't get is that sensitive people don't just play "princess" for fun; we actually can't stomach certain things and behaviors. For the people doing, saying, and making the things we can't stomach, it would be much more comfortable if they didn't have to deal with people like us. We burst their bubbles and question things, making them uncomfortable. For example, take the food industry. Of course, it makes some people millions of dollars to produce diet beverages, but the ingredients can destroy people's health.

You and I are not being too sensitive, we are just in touch with what our body and our psyche needs. My body needs food grown by Mother Earth in love, food that nourishes me, not through mass production, and my psyche needs honesty, not false advertising for capital gain—adding vitamins to diet sodas just doesn't cut it.

Be sensitive! I am inviting you to see your sensitivity as yet another sign of how well you are in touch with yourself when you allow yourself to be. Being so sensitive that in every moment you can feel what's good for you and what isn't. Living in that way is loving yourself and others, because you are connected and not numb. As a child you thought your feelings would kill you. By now, hopefully you know that suppressing your feelings and who you really are just might. Again, feelings are like a huge ocean. Waves come and go, and if you don't try to confine the ocean but learn how to ride the swell, you can have the best time surfing through your life.

EXERCISE

CLAIM YOUR SENSITIVITY

Tune in and learn what your system can handle and what it can't. Make sure you provide a safe space for yourself by becoming aware of your boundaries. Be respectful of yourself. Practice communicating your limits in a loving way. Know that your needs count. Be the first one to take them seriously.

LESSON for Day Six

SEXUALITY, CREATIVITY, AND LIFE FORCE

Today we look at sexuality, because—let's not kid ourselves—sex is essential to our lives.

Sexuality. For the longest time, I couldn't even say the word. My throat would get dry and I wished I could become invisible whenever the subject was broached. Having sex was extremely difficult unless I was severely drugged or drunk. I couldn't understand why God had cursed humanity so badly. I heard my parents and other people talk about how sex was like food for grownups. They needed it and enjoyed it; some even seemed to think it was the most fun thing in life. Parents neglected their children to do it, and children spied on their parents to get a glimpse. To me it was one, huge unsolvable mystery.

On drugs, I did have some experiences of utter bliss and oneness, but mostly my passion, if there was any, came into conflict with my traumatic past.

On the rare occasions I could connect to the force that allowed me to merge into oneness with another, I remembered who I truly was and am. I felt so open, so fearless, and so free. Eventually I came to the conclusion that God gave sex to people as a means for having a taste of enlightenment without us having actually arrived there yet. It kindles our desire to be in that high state and also is a reassurance that enlightenment is attainable by normal human beings and not just 100-year-old fasting yogis.

As I got older, I realized that what men (and women) do, under the disguise of sexuality, has nothing to do with the life-giving force of sexual energy. The sexual force itself is neither good nor bad, it is a mighty force that can be used both ways, life-giving and life-destroying. It can lead us to utter bliss or utter suffering.

What makes the difference is how you bring your consciousness to it. When you consciously use sexual energy, it sustains and fulfills you.

Some of my clients subconsciously draw the conclusion that sex is evil, and thus expel it from their life. Without sexual energy, you are cut off from your vital force. It's like cutting off the oxygen line for a deep sea diver—you are lucky if you survive. By denying this energy, you also deny your body, because it is with and through your body that you feel sexual energy.

I want to share something important with you here, a dilemma most of my clients have faced but don't allow themselves to think or talk about, because it's another taboo.

They remember feeling sexual and having sexual pleasure at the age that the abuse occurred. The abuse itself might have given their body feelings of pleasure, but their mind kept telling them that having pleasure in a situation like sexual abuse is wrong. And because their body experienced pleasure in such a twisted situation, they do not allow their bodies to have pleasure ever again. They deny themselves from feeling any sexual pleasure at all.

This is exactly what Peter Levine, the author and therapist I mentioned in Week 5, talks about. Think for a minute what would have happened if you had given in to your body and surrendered to its pleasure at the time of the abuse. Would you still have been traumatized? I do not know the answer, but what I do know is that we have to allow ourselves to ask these questions. We have to allow ourselves to ask, *Did I experience pleasure while I was abused?* And if the answer is yes, you should not be ashamed. You were a child and you didn't have a choice. Now, as an adult without that shame, you can use the memory to re-access the pleasure you felt by allowing yourself to feel in your body what you felt then.

What I have just shared is quite a stretch for most. But it does bring you closer to the truth and the freedom you are seeking. The more you are willing to reenter your body, the more you will allow and reconnect with vital sexual energy and your true essence.

KUNDALINI AWAKENING

In Hindu mythology, the sexual energy or life force is called *Kundalini*. Kundalini is seen as a snake that sleeps at the base of your spine and waits to be awakened to transform your consciousness. If you have taken yoga classes or some other Eastern practices, you might already be familiar with this concept and also have an energetic experience of it in your body.

Being in your body and owning your sexuality makes you strong and healthy. Not just strong in a physical sense, but strong in all areas, because you have your body's sensory system available to make decisions. Your real *yes* and *no* is always to be found within your body. Feeling your sexual energy means that you are home, that you are in your body. When someone is home, they can protect their home. As long as you are checked out and disconnected, energies and people can intrude and cause you harm.

Dance has always been my saving grace. Even in my darkest hours, dance allowed me to escape my self-made prison. Music touches the emotions. Moving to music allows you to express feelings and release energy that is otherwise stuck in your system. I continue to feel most alive while and after dancing, and of course after heart connected love-making. When I am by myself, dancing brings me out of my head and into direct experience. It brings me back into my body. I breathe, and my body produces heat.

I am sure you have experienced these moments too, moments in which time seemed irrelevant and a big smile crept over your face while you sunk into bliss. My goal in life is to feel connected and to have a life like I feel when I am dancing. Also, again my theory is that God gave us sex and dance, so we could get a glimpse of enlightenment without having to be saints. I know that for me, the best medicine is to dance. Drum music is the best, all by myself with no one watching. Connecting to earth below and sky above.

When I move, I am also reminded of my past, the past I don't remember consciously but can still feel in my bones. The past where I am the shaman going into a trance with the rhythm of the beat. The past of Serbia and Hungary and the Gypsy blood that mingled with the blood of my family. I touch them all in this magical way.

EXERCISE

KUNDALINI MEDITATION

Today you get to move again. I have recorded a "Kundalini meditation" that I use as a tool to reconnect with my body. You can find the recording and instructions for how to do it at www. BlossomBook.com/recordings.

Do this meditation as often as you like. Afterwards, journal about the changes you are experiencing.

LESSON
for Day Seven

WEEK SIX IN REVIEW

Being home and in your body and owning all of who you are is a prerequisite for having the intimacy and fulfillment you are longing for. This week might have been the time in the journey when you notice your openness to a relationship with another, or if you are in a relationship already, you might notice that relationship shifting. It might also be the time where you notice a shift in how you want to live your life. You might start to think about how you can realize your dream and allow yourself to make it happen. All of this is happening because you are starting to own all of who you are, which was the theme for this past week.

In Week Six, you learned that:

1. *When trauma happens, energy gets stuck in your nervous system and literally changes your physical makeup.*

2. *In order to thaw frozen, stuck energy, you have to be "in your body".*

3. *Your body is your gateway to your power and aliveness.*

4. *Only when you are home can you be safe and connected with another.*

So far, the journey has mostly been about you and your inner changes. The next and last step on this journey is to take what you have learned as your transformed self out into the world and let the world have it—your gifts and your love and light.

EXERCISE

REFLECT BACK

Reflect back on Week Six of your Blossom Journey. Take out your journal and write your answers to these questions: *What was most helpful to you in this week's lessons? What kinds of shifts can you already see within yourself and in the beliefs you have been holding? What is starting to change in your life?*

Write what comes to you.

Week Seven
MEET THE WORLD AND YOUR
BELOVED IN WHOLENESS

Take a moment here to celebrate yourself, because you have made it this far! You have arrived at Step 7, the last week of the Blossom Journey. This last step really is the launching pad for your ongoing journey of love and life. By now, you should notice some bigger shifts taking place in your life. You should notice new people, ideas, opportunities, and resources that are coming to support you.

At this point on your journey you may be asking yourself the question: *What does life and partnership look like when I am integrated, the full expression of my authentic self, and living my dream?*

When I asked myself that question, after searching for wholeness and peace for what was then half of my life, I realized that what I was longing for was not complete independence, but true intimacy. I desired true intimacy with my life, my work, in my family, and all my relationships. I knew that being an "integrated woman" didn't mean I was to "be my own man." I had a sense that being integrated meant I could be at peace just being a woman, "the other half of the sky," as John Lennon in his song "Woman" refers to us.

This is why the last step of the Blossom Journey is dedicated to the exploration of a healthy relationship between either a man and a woman, or same-sex partners. Between the feminine and the masculine, inside as well as outside of yourself and related to that, the fulfillment of your true purpose. I have come to believe that we all have a shared purpose, which is that each of us should become a living expression of our dream, the dream that brings us the most joy and pleasure. When you are living your dream, you give the greatest gift you can give. You then give others the permission to live their dream, too.

In my experience, and the experience of the many women I've helped on this journey, getting to a place where we could allow ourselves to move in the direction of manifesting our dream was only possible after we allowed ourselves to reconnect to our true feminine essence and nature. When we as women do that, miracles happen. Joseph Campbell, the great mythologist, writer and lecturer was absolutely right when he stated the often-quoted wisdom: "Follow your bliss, and the universe will open doors for you where there were only walls." I know that when we are in harmony, when male and female are in harmony, there is peace. Peace within and peace on earth.

Lesson for Day One

Man and Woman

Let's start this week by looking at the relationship between women and men. When you are in a relationship, as you learned, your chosen one becomes your mirror, and if you are not in a relationship, then the absence of a relationship becomes your mirror. What do you see when you look into that mirror—Do you see harmony or dissonance?

Either way, it tells you the state of your internal affairs. It tells you whether you are in wholeness and harmony or whether you are not.

Man and woman. Two halves of the same sky. A constant dance. Different make-ups, yet the same longing ultimately to be whole through the complement of the other. Men and women—wars have been fought in the name of love, poems have been written, and songs sung. Hearts broken, children made. The dance goes on.

Not long ago, the roles of the sexes were clearly defined. Men would go out and hunt and be the breadwinners. Women would stay home and take care of the children and be the housewives. Our grandmothers and mothers were one of the first generations of women allowed to wear dresses or pants, whatever was their liking.

Partnerships were silent agreements of dependence. Men relied on women for taking care of the house and children and for sex; women relied on men for status, protection, and the provision of basic necessities. For most women, it was true that if they didn't have a man, especially after they had children, it was almost impossible to survive. Not long ago, a woman became pregnant many times in her life and had many children, of which not all survived. Between being pregnant and caring for the children, there was not much time left for her to go out and be the breadwinner. The man needed to do that, or else the family was lost. I am not saying that men and women didn't love each other, but it was a dependent and probably often pain-filled love.

Women often felt suppressed, used, and like they were giving all of themselves (and often they did). They had no time or space to consider their own needs which they sacrificed for a secure survival and maybe love in return. As time went on, and a woman's survival became less based on having a man to take care of her, she still would give and give and give. It's engraved in our genes.

Soon women started having choices, having time and space to consider what they wanted, and men started to be confused and annoyed by the ever changing moods of their women. They started to feel restricted and restrained in the name of love. Both men and women longed for more freedom and more love at the end of the day.

Finally, with the feminist movement, women gained more rights and more liberties. Women became independent and no longer needed men for protection, status, and money. They put on the pants, climbed up the corporate ladder, and started smoking like factory smokestacks. Men, happy about the women loosening their needy grip on them, rejoiced, relaxed and stopped providing. Women still had the babies; women still did all the care-taking. Women now did it all. Women had become independent of men, not needing them anymore to survive and to bring up the next generation. Women started to lose their beauty, their radiance and joy, because the responsibilities of daily life started to weigh them down. Both women and men got lost in the new state of things.

And here we are today. Many men have lost their manliness, their sense of purpose and direction that their clearly defined roles as providers and protectors once gave them. Women, overwhelmed from doing it all, have lost their radiance due to all the burdens of their worldly responsibilities. The result of this equalization for the genders is that men and women live together in fairly arranged 50/50 relationships, where each can be independent of the other. But the truth is that each is longing for something so much deeper.

Most of my clients have been through co-dependent romantic relationships with passionate love-making but torturous fights and dependencies. When they got married they made sure that *that* wouldn't happen again. They chose a marriage with less passion but equal rights and responsibilities. No more roller coaster rides and no more drama!

For most of them, the arrangement worked until the kids got a little older, and they had time to think again. Then the longing for something else could no longer be ignored. They blame their partner, and their partners blame them for not being loving, not wanting to be intimate, and for not being happy. They get out of an ultra-dependent relationship and make sure it will never happen again. Instead of relaxing into their feminine nature, they make efforts to outdo men. They work, they make money, and they tell him what to do. They become very focused and directional. They unknowingly start living more from their masculine side than from their feminine side.

You could wonder now, what is so wrong with that? There is nothing "wrong" with it, it's just that it diminishes the attraction and polarity between the sexes, and it is not very healthy for a female body to run on male energy. Being in a healthy partnership, two people are like two poles. One is the more masculine and one is the more feminine. Ideally, the person with the naturally more feminine essence is the feminine pole, and the one with the more masculine natural essence is the masculine pole. But in most relationships today, the poles have gotten reversed.

The ones with the feminine essences, meaning you and I, are not living our natural essence, because of what has happened to us through male domination. We decided subconsciously that it was safer to become "our own man," thus strongly animating our masculine energy. The number of single moms who either decided or apparently had no other choice than to father and mother their children is proof of this as well. And the "new" generation of men is so unsure about their direction, they don't want to assert themselves or make decisions, but choose to be airy-fairy and non-committal, understanding and soft. In essence, they are living more strongly in their feminine essence, because they didn't have a role model for what true masculinity looks like.

In our society, the female essence is seen as inferior, because it is less directional, changing and more open. The female is the life force itself, it's incalculable. Men, since the beginning of time, have tried to out-think life. None of us like the unknown, because it makes us feel out of control. We all want to know what's going on. We want to feel somewhat in control, and so we retreat into our minds where we have the capacity to plan. Having a plan gives a false sense of security and makes things appear predictable. It doesn't matter that it is a false sense, because we take it as reality. We feel in control when we have a plan.

The feminine heart doesn't need to plan. It trusts that there is already a divine plan behind everything. It flows with life wherever life takes it. It is the unknown itself, because it is ever changing. In a society that is tainted by fear, the unknown is not what is valued. The mind, the one that we think can out-think life, is in charge to our disadvantage, unfortunately. Because the masculine essence is more directional, it takes much less effort for men to amass money, and because they are physically stronger they can also, with their directed physical force, suppress the feminine. Women think that their only chance of standing their ground is to defend themselves and get into a fight, do as the men do. It's good to stand up and show boundaries, but it increases the sum of male energy on planet earth, which throws off the natural balance.

My theory is that when integrated men and women raise their sons and daughters in a way that those children can keep their hearts open and be in their true sexual essence, the world will slowly shift into a world of less fear. A world where the feminine and the masculine are both honored for their gifts and equally safe to express them.

As mentioned before, currently our world is out of balance, because we all have bought into the myth that the mind is far superior to the heart. The saying goes that knowledge is power. I want to challenge that and say *love is power*. The subconscious belief is that the male is far more able to survive then the female. Survival of the fittest. Well, if we all fight for our lives, then no one will be left. How about trying the feminine way of everyone being vulnerable? Then there would be no need for fight, and survival of the fittest would be an obsolete way of life. It takes a change in your consciousness and in that of every woman.

When you realize that vulnerability and surrender does not mean weakness, that being guided by your heart doesn't make you inferior, that it's just a myth cultivated for thousands and thousands of years, then you are doing your part in bringing balance not only back to your own self but to the entire world.

EXERCISE

EXPLORE YOUR BELIEFS

Today explore the beliefs that you hold about the feminine and the masculine essences in our world. For example, *a man should make more money than a woman.* Find as many as you can and write them down in your journal.

Lesson for Day Two

THE THREE LEVELS OF RELATIONSHIP

Today we are going even deeper in our understanding of the relationship between women and men. There are three levels of relationship I want to talk about: *co-dependent, equality*, and *true intimacy*. David Deida, an American author who writes about the sexual and spiritual relationship between men and women, talks about this in his books that have been published in 25 languages. Most of us have lived through co-dependent relationships and boring 50/50 equality style ones, and are now at a point where we are looking to create a new paradigm. Our hearts yearn for a relationship of true intimacy.

As women, our deepest longing is to be, feel, and have love. To have a relationship with our lover and a life that is deeply fulfilling on all levels. Fulfilling on the physical (yes, I am talking sex here), the emotional, energetic, and spiritual levels.

Most women seek love first in dependent relationships. You fall in love, you're on cloud nine or even cloud 100, and you give everything you have to the guy, yourself included, just to gain the love that you feel you never got. And then you fall – you fall so deep, it hurts. You fall as deep as you are high. Then there comes a point in your life when you have had it. No more giving to the guys. Enough of the drama of co-dependency – you are no longer willing to put up with the draining, up-and-down roller coaster ride. You want equilibrium and stability.

Next, you may have achieved a more balanced relationship with a man—one that feels healthier, one where both of you are equals—and you think you have arrived. But you soon realize something is still missing. The relationship feels nice and stable, and there is no drama, but also no passion. In the co-dependent relationship you fought a lot but at least you also had passionate make-up sessions. You want the passion but without the drama. With the guy you are with, that seems out of reach. At some point, you decide that this whole love thing isn't worth it. That some people are just lucky in love, they found Mr. Right and the love of their lives, but it isn't meant for you. Rather than letting yourself get pulled off track, you put all your focus on your business and career or your children and seek to be fulfilled by money and success, or the happy smiles of your little ones. And you are—for a while.

In my late teens, I met the man who became my "big love." I would do everything for him. I loved him so much that I would give up myself completely. I stayed with him for almost six years. It was classic. He didn't really want to be in relationship. He wanted to have fun with the boys. I wanted him so badly that I tolerated a lot—not hearing from him for days, finding him drunk on park benches in the morning, and then giving him my money so he could go party again. I even tolerated being called every name in the book when he was drunk, because the attention and love I got from him when he was sober or came to his senses was the sweetest thing. Never before had I felt so close or connected with anyone. I was sure he was my soul mate. It took him throwing a glass at me in an angry fit and demanding that I take the morning after pill for me to leave. Even then, it took me almost a decade to get over him.

Today I know that the reason I felt so close and was so addicted to this person was that he triggered in me all my core wounds. He made me feel the way I knew how to feel, the way I felt when I was little. I am eternally grateful to him, because he woke me up in a way. I know that on a soul level we are deeply connected, but in this lifetime we were not meant to remain partners and raise a family together.

I'm guessing that you can relate to how emotionally draining such a relationship can be. A relationship like that takes it all from you and leaves nothing. As long as you are in a co-dependent relationship, you have no energy to fulfill your own life's purpose and your heart's deepest desires.

I believe the truth is that love is meant for everyone, not just for some. The truth also is that when you don't have love in your life, it's not the "right guy" that's missing. What's missing is your deep surrender to love and life itself. When you are connected to love, when you follow your bliss, you are free to leave situations that aren't good for you and choose the ones that are. In order for you to get to a place where you can create a relationship that doesn't drain you or bore you, you need to grow beyond your limiting ways of relating.

Over the course of the next few days, we will look at how you can grow in this area. One of the first steps is to become aware of how you give in a relationship. Are you giving in a co-dependent way, meaning giving to get love in return? Or are you giving in an independent way, giving but not really giving fully? Or are you giving in a way that is neither of these, but a way that fulfills you?

Exercise

How Do You Give?

Pay attention to your giving. As women, we often confuse total self-sacrifice (co-dependent giving) for love. Is it really love when we give every little bit of energy that we have to the people around us?

How do you feel inside when you are giving, giving, giving? Do you feel full or empty? If you feel empty, then you most likely have been giving in order to get back. Real love only gives to become fuller, to expand on its own. Pay attention to the moments you give and feel fuller and the moments you give and feel empty. Notice the difference and pay attention. In the evening, write about your discoveries in your journal.

LESSON for Day Three

YOUR MALE AND FEMALE SIDES

Today we will look at the male and female aspects you have within yourself to find out how you can come to a place of peace.

Yin and yang, sun and moon, earth and sky, plus and minus—polarity is everywhere.

Being born on earth is being born into polarity. Out of oneness consciousness into individual consciousness. Into you and me. Me and the other. Duality is not just outside of us but inside of us as well.

In earlier weeks of your Blossom Journey, you learned about the many different parts that make up the entirety of who you are. Another way of looking at yourself is to recognize the different energies that are flowing within and through you. Some of these energies are connected to your feminine and some to your masculine side. All of us have both, each with a unique combination.

Your masculine side drives you to action. It's the part of you that makes plans and then executes them. It is expressed as your analytical mind and your inner judge, the parts of you that want to be free. Your feminine side is that part of you that is chaotic, nurturing, hunting for love, and wanting to relate and connect. As you unite these two principals or two energies within yourself, so does humanity. As much as you couldn't exist without one of the two, humanity can't exist without both being present.

Gaining awareness of your own make up and the ability to turn on one mode more than the other when needed is very useful when dancing in relationships.

The male always seeks freedom. The ultimate freedom is reached in death, where we surpass all of our earthly confinements. Throughout life, men, or the masculine aspect in you, engages in activities that give you this death-like freedom, a relief from yourself and your burdens. Orgasms give you that as does raging in violence, watching TV, and losing oneself in philosophy-land.

A man abusing a woman is yet another attempt of the male energy to feel free. It's a very short-lived freedom, which the man's soul and the soul of his entire family pays for dearly. Men who abuse women are not conscious enough to realize that what they are seeking is freedom, and that this freedom never lies in destruction. In their unconscious state, they don't realize that it's not a woman that is restricting them but the conditionality of life. True freedom lies, in my opinion, in the realization of our true essence.

As much as a man is seeking unconditional love through the pursuit of freedom via death-like experiences, women are looking for unconditional love through connection, hoping to be completely fulfilled by it.

True sexual union is an experience of total freedom and unconditional love. It is an experience that fills and frees you at the same time. If you have decided that sex and pleasure is wrong or evil, because it has caused you so much harm, you have no way of experiencing true union with another or with yourself, and thus no real means of truly feeling fulfillment.

When this is the case, you come up with substitutes that are supposed to fulfill you. Like food. The full belly becomes a substitute for the deep loving you are craving. But you long to be loved and experience unconditional love. Food just doesn't cut it. And thus for many of us, a vicious cycle begins.

You eat in an attempt to feel fuller and have more love. You feel full and happy for a moment. But after that moment you come down to reality and feel even emptier than before. Because it feels so uncomfortable, after a short while, you talk yourself into forgetting about the "coming off" period, and you eat again, because it lets you feel full and good for a moment.

I know about this, because it was my fate for many years.

You might think, *If I just had more sex, the craving for food will go away.* But as long as sex is just an empty means of getting something, your heart will still be left in longing. Just like with the food, you will feel happy and fulfilled for maybe 15 minutes at best, and then the crash begins again.

And then all you are left with is your anger. I have come to understand that our anger ultimately is the sadness that's covered over. The sadness is about not allowing ourselves to live our feminine side, that side that wants to be filled. That side that wants to pursue pleasure and joy.

EXERCISE

WHICH SIDE ARE YOU ON?

Today observe yourself and start to become aware of which side, masculine or feminine, you predominately come from when interacting with others. Also notice what the particular situations are that you are in when interacting. Where do you generally feel more comfortable, in your softness and femininity or in your direction-oriented masculine side? Explore the question: *When does it serve me to be more masculine and when more feminine?* Reflect on your day in the evening and journal about it.

Lesson for Day Four

BALANCING THE FEMININE
AND THE MASCULINE

You would think that balance between male and female meant that each of us, regardless of being a man or a woman, has our inner female and inner male flowing equally with female and male energy.

But this is not the case. Think about what happens when two polarities are equaled. They come to neutralize each other, and neutrality is not the same as balance.

Instead, true balance looks more like this: A woman is in balance when her natural female energy is dominant, and a man is in balance when his natural male energy is dominant. (Of course, there are women who have a more natural masculine energy and men that have a more natural female energy, but they constitute the exception. If you are one of them, just reverse the gender in what I am saying, and read on!)

The world is in balance when women live more dominantly in their feminine energy and men in their masculine. As mentioned, right now on the planet, a lot of women are unbalanced because they have animated their masculine energy more than their feminine in an attempt to be like men and therefore gain more rights, respect, and safety. And yes, many woman have gained more rights and independence but at the cost of their balance and health. We want balance and we want to be strong in our femininity, because our true power lies in who we really are.

Do you have the sense that only when you are able to relax into your true nature will you be able to experience what you are longing for in life and intimacy?

How do you open to love and stay there? This question must become your daily mantra. The first step was to commit yourself to love, as you did at the beginning of this journey. You didn't commit to being with any one person in particular. You committed to exploring what love truly is. Your lovers and partners only serve as mirrors.

I teach my clients over and over again that when there is a conflict, it is never about the other person. Even though your mind makes it appear to be so. It is always about love, about you being open and in wholeness or closed down and in fragmentation. Love always knows what's right. When you are committed to love, you know that love is an open heart. So when you are closing down, you are not fulfilling your commitment to love. It's about you feeling your heart and knowing what it feels like when you close down in protection.

And when that happens, when you recognize that you have closed down or that you are about to close down to unconditionally be with your heart and feelings, there is no need to yell or scream. Breathe and feel until the closeness reverts to openness.

If you are committed to love, you can open up again no matter what is happening. You know to stop listening to the noise in your mind and dive deep into yourself, your center, your heart. The essential conflict that we all experience is the battle between the mind and the heart.

Again, we live in the world of polarity. That is the nature of being here. Polarity is created through your internal energies of masculine and feminine, in other words through your heart and your mind. Neither is good or bad in and of themselves. Both have their rightful place.

You want to be free of your mind's dictatorship and your heart's fear. Dictatorship and fear aren't true qualities of either the mind or the heart. Also, emotionally based decisions aren't necessarily decisions made in your best interest, even though you didn't make them with your mind. Here is how you can know that you are on the right path, meaning the one that brings you peace.

The path that brings you peace is the path where you use the heart in its right place and the mind in its right place. This is the path that is in alignment with who you are and lets you flow through life without added drama.

You might have had the tendency to want to get rid of your mind or at least the voices that cause you mental confusion. But here is the deal. When your emotional imprints are integrated, your mental confusion stops as well, because there is no need for your old stories to be told again and again. You know in your core that you are safe. Whenever you catch yourself trapped in your mind, trying to think over and over again of possibilities and future happenings, trying to plan rather than embrace life, you know you are not using your mind in the way it was meant to be used.

This is what I mean by saying when you don't use your mind or heart in the right way, you end up in conflicts with others or in an inner war with yourself. Whenever you can't focus on your work or be present in life because your emotions have a tight grip on you, you know that you are using your heart in the wrong way. Or better said, what you are experiencing are not true feelings but old imprints that feel like they come from your heart because your heart is connected to your feeling capacity.

When you are afraid, your heart is most likely closed down. Only when your heart is open can it serve you and its purpose. So feelings do play an important role in distinguishing whether you are really following your heart (the right path), or whether it is an old imprint.

When you feel open and good in your body, when you feel your *yes*, which we talked about earlier, then you can be sure you are in alignment and balance. Then you are using your heart and mind for their intended purpose. This to me is what true balance of the masculine and feminine within us is really all about.

EXERCISE

FAKE IT 'TIL YOU MAKE IT

Today, when some event or person triggers you, ask yourself the question: *What would love do or say?* And wait for the answer.

If you are really triggered and your emotions are cooking, step into the bathroom or another private place and fake a smile for 17 seconds. Your reptilian brain doesn't know the difference; your facial muscle flexion will trigger an endorphin release to help you calm down, giving you access to other emotions and reactions than just fight-or-flight.

Fake it until you make it. Pretend you are Jesus or Mary Magdalena or Buddha, or any other unconditional loving being to whom you have an affinity. Intuit what they would say or do if in your situation, and then do that.

Lesson
for Day Five

Moving Into Your Feminine Power

Before we explore what true feminine power is and how you can get into your true power, I find it necessary to first look at empowerment. More specifically, let's look at the women's empowerment movement, because it is my experience that there is a lot of confusion around female power and empowerment. It is also my experience that women's empowerment is often connected to a lot of anger. All the female anger, to be specific.

Women's empowerment has become such a catchphrase today. Fighting for your own rights as a woman could easily seem like the way out of your situation, and sometimes we do have to fight. But the ego is very clever. It takes on the voice of your cheerleader, but in the end its agenda is to keep you safe. The safety that the ego wants is the safety based on a 2-year-old's needs and not necessarily what is really to your greatest benefit.

Fighting for anything will never bring us closeness and bliss. The question for me became, *Is the woman's empowerment movement really helping us as women when it comes to fulfilling our greatest purpose and moving into our true power?*

Of course, you shouldn't stay in an abusive relationship or situation, but often in empowerment talks or groups, it is suggested that you become a warrior. That you fight for your rights, that you show the guy, the boss, the "male opponent" who you are and that you are at least as strong if not stronger. You want to show that you don't need him.

Power often is attributed to male energy, and so in pursuing it, we become more masculine because we do not understand what true feminine power is. Masculine power doesn't equal feminine power. Masculine and feminine powers are equally powerful in degree, but very different in their nature.

In the end you work against yourself and against your true nature when you go about empowerment in a way that is driven by anger.

There were times in my life when I was so filled with anger towards men that I wished I could cut their balls off (excuse the language). Many of my clients tell me they had those moments as well. These days, when I am looking down at my sleeping son, I wonder what must have happened to make men do cruel things beyond comprehension. He is such a bundle of innocence and love. What has society done to little boys that they are in so much pain when they become grown men?

As a mother with a son, the greatest gift you can give him is to heal your anger towards men, so you are capable of raising him to become a man who isn't traumatized by a traumatized mother and a missing father. So that he can be a man who is connected to his heart and balanced in the feminine and masculine expression of himself.

There is nothing more detrimental to a child's soul than a mother's ambiguous love. Most men living in our times grew up with a father that either went to war or himself had a father who went to war, saw awful things, did awful things, and possibly even died in a war. Many men today were raised by a single mom. The point I am making is that a lot of men grew up and are growing up without their fathers being present. From the Family Constellation work, I know that the greatest pain a child's soul suffers is not having both parents or not being allowed to love both parents equally. It literally creates a split within.

Most men were not allowed to open their hearts and let their true essence shine. This is changing bit by bit. Men are going through their own variation of a Blossom Journey right now.

The question still remains, *What is true female empowerment, and what does it mean as a woman to be in your power?*

I want to tell you another story from my own life. Something that just recently happened and truly opened my eyes.

As I told you, I had been married for about five years when I decided one night that I had enough of this arrangement. An arrangement by which it seemed to me that I was losing out all the time. A dynamic in which I constantly felt disempowered and overpowered by him. My needs never counted, so it seemed, and the only way I could see my needs getting met was to leave and find someone else who was not overpowering me and could hear my needs.

The next morning, much to my husband's surprise, I took off my wedding band and gave it back to him. I felt good, I felt strong, I felt tough, I felt like finally I was playing the game his way, where I was no longer the one getting hurt, now he was. Now he could feel what it felt like to have a broken heart and a crumbled spirit.

All my girlfriends and even my mom were congratulating me for my courage and for my new found freedom. Their enthusiasm was almost scary. Shouldn't they have been voting for me to keep my family together?

As I shared with you, I didn't get off the proverbial hook quite so easily. God gave us the baby. I had wanted a second child very badly. He not so much, another issue in our lives where I felt overpowered and out of control.

We stayed separated for most of my pregnancy. At first, my masculine side had a blast. I had more energy than ever, made more money than in a long time, looked and felt attractive, and even had some casual sex, just like the guys.

At five months pregnant, I found out I was carrying a boy. At six months pregnant, I really didn't feel like pretending to be my own man anymore. It felt so very counter-intuitive to what was going on in my body. Seven months into my pregnancy, I surrendered into my husband's loving arms, because I needed someone I could trust to lean on and to hold me. That moment felt oddly enough like one of the most courageous moments in my life. If someone was watching from the outside, it might have looked like a poor weak woman was simply losing it, needing to be held by someone strong.

But what was happening in reality was, for the first time, I was letting my guard down fully and standing there emotionally naked in front of my man. Soft, open, and vulnerable, and at the same time empowered in a true feminine way, saying, "I do not want to do this alone. I do not want to pretend I can be both a man and a woman at the same time any longer."

I need you to be the man.

The moment I became soft and open, I didn't feel over-powered anymore. When I took my place as a woman, he didn't have to fight with me anymore, and he was finally allowed to do what he wanted to do, which was to just love and support me.

I came away from this experience with two lessons about empowerment: One, empowerment is about becoming your true self, and as a woman part of your true self is soft and gentle, loving and vulnerable; and two, empowerment doesn't necessarily mean you are strong enough to do it all by yourself, but it means that you know that you need another and that you are not afraid to honor and voice that need.

I can hear you thinking at this point, *but what about co-dependency and neediness? Where does one start and the other end?*

And yes you are right—it is a very fine energetic line. But what I am talking about here has nothing to do with co-dependency. It has everything to do with being a healthy, whole man or woman (or in gay relationships, as I understand it, the one who takes on being the female and the other who takes on being the male), together forming a balanced relationship, and having the potential to experience themselves as close to completeness and true love as is possible in human form.

Your true power also comes from reconnecting to your heart and remembering the dreams you once had. The truth in my heart was that I wanted to have a healthy and happy family. I remember being little and wondering why the grownups had such a hard time being together—in my child's mind, living as a family was easy. Just love one another.

When you follow your heart and listen to what it is telling you about how you can make yourself happy, you are then in power. Again, the pursuit of what brings you pleasure and joy is the key that unlocks your magnificence.

When you are connected to your essence, you are in your power. You are in your true power when, *yes,* you can be on your own, but at the same time you know you need others. When you can live and allow both truths, that is the meaning of empowerment.

EXERCISE

FINDING YOUR TRUE POWER

Reflect on the question: When do I feel my true power? Observe yourself throughout the day. In the evening, journal about your discoveries.

LESSON for Day Six

TRUE INTIMACY

Today, the final lesson in Step 7, the final step of your Blossom Journey, we are going to dive deeper into the exploration of true intimacy.

Oftentimes when you hear the word intimacy, what comes to mind immediately is sex. To me, sex is an aspect of true intimacy, but true intimacy goes far beyond that one moment of bliss. It is absolutely possible to experience a very intimate moment during sex but also by just looking into the eyes of a stranger or a newborn baby.

The kind of intimacy I am referring to is a state that is continually practiced and experienced in relationship to one specific human being. The one we have committed to practicing true intimacy with. True intimacy between a man and a woman can only evolve if there is a mutual feeling of trust and safety. True intimacy requires us to be fully present in our sexual essence, in our life force, and to be living with an open heart.

Those of us who have been sexually traumatized, as you learned, have given up our true sexual nature. Because we are women, most of us naturally have a feminine sexual essence. Approximately 10% of us have a more masculine sexual essence and 10% have a more neutral sexual essence. Almost 100% of us who have experienced sexuality as a bad thing, have chosen to take on either a neutral or a masculine sexual mask to avoid becoming a target for masculine sexual energy.

A small percentage of us have chosen to become, at first glance, even more sexually feminine and to prostitute our bodies. This, in my opinion, is a false feminine sexuality, because in its essence it is a way to control and be in charge sexually. It is a very aggressive way to express oneself sexually. The masculine sexual essence is very directional and guiding. It's having sex as the men do.

The masculine essence also can be equated with thrusting forward, being goal-oriented, aggressive and assertive. The feminine sexual essence is flowing and opening in love. It is less directional and more all-inclusive. Where the masculine essence seeks to express itself through action, the feminine expresses itself through receiving.

For us women who have been hurt, it seems a very dangerous suggestion that we surrender ourselves to the masculine. Yet deep in our hearts we long for the safety to do just that.

Deep down in our core we long to be women in a safe world, not because we are the same as men and therefore not a target any longer, but because the masculine truly honors our love and softness. It needs and wants our soft love to survive and therefore protects it.

What can we as women do to move from our safe equality with men into our true essence?

True intimacy, whether we currently have a partner or not, requires of us that we risk being hurt again, that we risk not being our own man, that we risk giving freely.

That we open ourselves and receive all the love that is there. That we let our guard down and feel our heart, moment to moment.

It requires of us that rather than doing something to get love, as we did in our co-dependent relationships, or rather than attempting to give all the love that we really need ourselves, that we practice being love itself.

As I mentioned, I had taken off my wedding band and threw it in front of my man on the table, stating that our arrangement was no longer working, that I wasn't interested in our lukewarm equality marriage. When I did put my wedding band back on, I did it in commitment to being love itself. When I am an expression of love, I am expressing my true essence. When I am expressing my true essence, I am in my power. It is the same for you. My wedding band serves as a daily reminder of that commitment.

This is where you are coming full circle on the Blossom Journey. Remember in the beginning you were asked to commit to being love itself? I want to leave you with the question, *Did you?*

It was my intention that *Blossom* give you all the tools you need in order to keep that commitment, so that you, too, can be all that you came here to be, which is the wild, strong, gentle, powerful, and radiant woman you truly are.

EXERCISE

COMMITMENT REMINDER

Get creative and come up with a commitment reminder that clearly states your commitment to love. It could be a ring, a necklace or a note on the fridge. Make sure it is something that is visible and catches your attention often.

LESSON
for Day Seven
WEEK SEVEN IN REVIEW

You have come full circle in your Blossom Journey. In the seven weeks of the journey, you traveled out of your mind into your heart. You learned what it takes to integrate your pain, so you can stay present and open your heart. You not only have learned how to open your heart when you are safe and by yourself, but you have also learned and already started to practice what it takes to keep your heart open, no matter what.

In this final step, in Week Seven, you learned that:

1. *In order to have the deeply fulfilling relationship and life you say you want, it is necessary to relax into your true feminine nature.*

2. *Most of your relationship troubles have come from "reversed roles," the masculine and feminine forces being out of balance.*

3. *Practicing true intimacy is the dance of a real relationship today.*

4. *You are invited to go in the pursuit of pleasure.*

5. *A commitment reminder will help you navigate your path in the pursuit of true love, true power, and fulfilling relationships in life.*

Some journeys start with the first day and end with the last. Well, this is not one of them. The day you started walking this journey, you launched yourself into a new life. The seven weeks that have passed have now become your launching pad, leaving you equipped with everything you need in order to take off and create the magnificent life you so desire.

Exercise

Reflect Back

Reflect back on Week Seven of your Blossom Journey. Take out your journal and write your answers to these questions: *What was most helpful to you in this week's lessons? What kinds of shifts can you already see within yourself and in the beliefs you have been holding? What is starting to change in your life?*

Write what comes to you.

Where to Go from Here...

Before you go anywhere, turn around and look at the changes and transformations that have happened in your life since you started the journey. These changes and transformations all happened because you were willing to put in the work.

Take a breath and honor yourself for the deep commitment you have to love, to yourself, to your family, and to your lover.

You have learned a ton in the last seven weeks. There might be lessons and practices you want to take further by studying them on your own, like learning Non-Violent Communication, practicing dance and movement, or doing the Consciously Connected Breathing I introduced.

There might also be other things that you would like to explore further with the help of someone like me. You might want to come to one of my Family Constellation workshops or learn how to do the soul motions process. If you are a therapist yourself you might even want to learn how you can use some of what you have learned with your own clients. To book a Constellation or to find out how you can train with me, go to www.CarolinHauser.com.

No matter what you choose to do, pick five things from *Blossom* and integrate them into your daily life.

To keep your commitment strong and share your journey with fellow travelers, I have created a special Blossom Facebook Group where you can meet and connect with other women just like you. Find me on Facebook and ask me to connect you to that group. My Facebook page is Facebook.com/carolinhauser. I spend time there too, so if you have questions or feedback and comments, say hello and let me hear from you.

I wish you the best, most fulfilling and deeply enjoyable experiences in your continually *Blossoming* life!

About the Author

Carolin Hauser has been involved in the personal healing field for more than 15 years. She holds a degree in Naturopathic Medicine from Germany and is a Humanistic Psychotherapist and Family Constellation facilitator.

Carolin has the unique ability to hold the space for others, so that tremendous change and integration can occur. Beginning at the age of 11, Carolin endured more than 12 years of immense "soul pain," which manifested in eating disorders, addictive behavior, co-dependent relationships, and depression. Today, she knows that most of this pain was caused by the childhood sexual abuse she suffered.

After many short and unfulfilling relationships, and an almost destroyed marriage and family, Carolin needed to find a way to heal her own broken heart. This she did. Today she has reconciled her relationship with her husband and parents, and is teaching women all over the world how to release their trauma and create their "dream life" and relationships.

Carolin lives in beautiful Santa Barbara, California, with her husband and two beautiful children. She travels around the world, teaching and spreading the message of hope that an absolutely fulfilling life for trauma survivors is possible.

To receive Carolin's Blossom E-zine, subscribe today at www.CarolinHauser.com.

Recommended Resources

CAROLIN'S STUFF

To find out about Carolin's workshops and trainings go to:

www.CarolinHauser.com

WEBSITES

SCIENCE OF MIND CHURCH
www.unitedcentersforspiritualliving.org

CENTER FOR NON-VIOLENT COMMUNICATION (NVC)
www.cnvc.org

DAVID DEIDA
deida.info

RECOMMENDED READING

Creative Visualization by Shakti Gawain

The Power of Now by Eckart Tolle

Waking the Tiger: Healing Trauma: The Innate Capacity to Transform Overwhelming Experiences by Peter A. Levine

The Presence Process by Michael Brown

Return to Love by Marianne Williamson

Acknowledgments

My greatest thanks go to my parents, Christina Nett and Hans-Joachim Hauser, and all the ones in my family who came before me. Without them, I would not be here.

This book also would not have been possible without the unconditional support and love of my husband. Thank you so much, Daniel. Your support means the world to me.

Thank you Maja and Nouri, my children, for letting me write and do my work. I love you both so much.

Thank you to my sister, Anna-Lena Hauser, and all my soul sisters for believing in me and supporting me throughout this journey.

Thank you to my brother, David Hauser, for the design help and for just loving me the way I am. Thank you to all my soul brothers for your support.

Special thanks go to Christine Kloser, my "Book Midwife" who helped me birth this book into the world.

Thank you to Lynne Klippel for your continued support and belief in my book.

Thank you to Erin Boehme and Lia Grippo from Wildroots Forest School for giving me peace of mind: I always knew Maja was in such great care with you. Thank you to Varuna for taking such loving care of Nouri.

Thank you to Caroline Bamforth Firman for your support in helping me tackle the English language, and for helping me get all the little things done. Your help is greatly appreciated.

Thank you to Kimberly Hansen for cover graphics development, Viola Hauser for final cover graphic design and Clayton Smith for interior and final exterior design.

Thanks to Nancy Marriott of New Paradigm Writing and Editing Services for the manuscript's first edit. You captured my voice so well.

Thank you to Karen Arena and Linda Taylor for proofreading.

Heather Young, thank you for the final edit.

Without the Blossom Fundraiser, the publishing of *Blossom* would not have been possible. Thank you to all contributors and anonymous donors.

A special thanks goes to all the people of the "Seed" group, your financial contributions helped make *Blossom* possible.

Thank you Kimberly Burnham, Tricia Shaffer Martinez, Manisha Mehta, Linda Lee, Sharmin Manzarek, Mona Bhattacharya of www.Lumenoctave.com, Deborah Jane Wells of www.DJW-Lifecoach.com, Lilia Shoshanna Rae of www.lightlovetruthwisdom.com, and Bridgit Gooden of www.ctransformations.com for believing in this book and contributing so generously to it.

Thank you to all my clients, friends, and teachers, past and present; Osho, Amma, Michael Brown, Eckhart Tolle, Bert Hellinger, Dyrian and Joanna Benz-Chartrant, Miria Karin Jende and the entire TTA team. There are so many of you who helped me bring *Blossom* forth, so please excuse me if your name is not listed here. Just know I am very grateful in my heart for your support.

Paying it Forward

I deeply believe in not only talking the talk but also walking the walk. Therefore, I am committing 10% of all profits from *Blossom* towards two wonderful projects. These projects are helping children, both locally and globally, to grow up safe and to strive.

I chose these two projects because I personally know and admire the women behind them, and can absolutely vouch for their integrity and pureness of intention.

The first project is Project LIGHT Rwanda.

Here is what Lori Leyden, founder of Project LIGHT Rwanda, says: "Project LIGHT Rwanda is the world's first International Youth Healing, Leadership and Entreprenuership Program serving orphan genocide survivors. Since 2007 our small, all-volunteer organization, Create Global Healing, has conducted trauma healing work with thousands of orphan genocide survivors in Rwanda. But we knew that trauma healing wasn't enough, so we created Project LIGHT: Rwanda to nurture a whole new generation of young people who are able to heal, work and lead us into a peaceful future.

Our vision is to create Project LIGHT centers around the world, where young people receive emotional healing and training, real opportunities for economic independence and the freedom to become heart-centered leaders. We utilize advanced technology to have real-time interactions between these young people, students, donors and our visionary Resource Partners in the fields of education, healing arts, business and entrepreneurship. We also have created a business incubator to develop products and services that will make these Centers self-sustainable."

For more information please visit www.ProjectLIGHTRwanda.com and www.CreateGlobalHealing.org.

The second project that *Blossom* will support is the Wildroots Forest School.

Here is what Lia Grippo, the Founder and Director of this great program, says:

"What we love, we are likely to protect, and to love something we must know it. Wild Roots, a forest school located in Santa Barbara, CA, has been educating young children in Nature's classrooms since 1998. Using wild harvested materials in play and work, preschool and kindergarten students experience interdependence through all of their senses. The children are busy foraging, recognizing plants that can heal or harm us, tracking and observing animals, observing changes on the land, painting, drawing, crafting, and playing in nature's playground. Daily, the land offers a host of new adventures to spark the natural curiosity and imagination of each child.

Wildroots Forest School provides a safe and nurturing environment for children, so that they might strive and blossom in today's fast paced world."

By purchasing *Blossom*, you helped and contributed to both of these amazing projects.

Thank you!

Made in the USA
San Bernardino, CA
17 March 2016